GET YOUR KNEE
OFF OUR NECKS

GET YOUR KNEE
OFF OUR NECKS

I0161463

FREDERICK MONDERSON

1

FREDERICK MONDERSON

Get Your Knee Off Our Backs Photo. At the "Tribute to Prof. George Simmonds" at the Victoria 5 Theater in Harlem, "Young" Fred Monderson sat at the feet of his heroes Dr. Ben-Jochannan and with Prof. George Simmonds in full-chiefly regalia, among others.

ISBN – 978-1-61023-070-4
LCCN – 2020910675

Get Your Knee Off Our Necks Photo – "Mother Africa protects her Children!"

GET YOUR KNEE
OFF OUR NECKS
TABLE OF CONTENTS

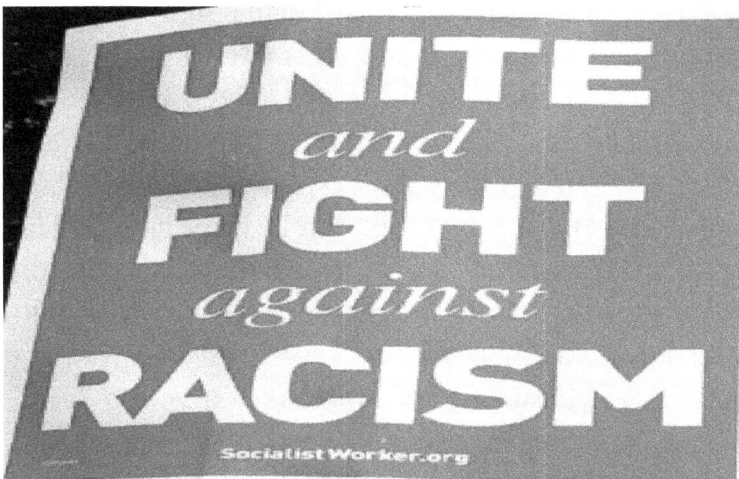

Get your Knee off Our Necks – Photo –

GET YOUR KNEE OFF OUR NECKS is a
DEMAND that not only speaks to the condition
under which George Floyd was mercilessly
murdered, but truly reflects the harsh reality that
recognizes Africans freed from enslavement in
America have for long been victimized particularly
by ingrained institutional practices. W.E.B. DuBois
reminded, "This is how the system was designed" to
control and mark the African held in bondage. This
treatment, designed as it is from the inception,
encouraged a particular stigma associated with
being Black in this country profoundly epitomized
in the recent Central Park incident of a young White
woman, not wearing a mass and walking her dog
without a leash, though signs were posted; she was
being recorded by an innocent Black man 'bird-

GET YOUR KNEE
OFF OUR NECKS

watching' at a distance from her, yet insisting she keep her distance in this time of Pandemic. Here, her actions underscore the psychological trauma and devastation meted out and represented in her and so many others' thinking, "All I have to say is, 'A Black man is harassing and threatening my life' and the police will come instantly to take care of him, in whatever manner.'" This is the fear that haunts daily life for the Black, especially, young man and woman. Sandra Bland, Breonna Taylor, Eleanor Bumpers, etc.

Previously, though now trending, a young Black man, Elijah McClain, wearing a 'ski-mask' was stopped because he "looked suspicious" and, in three days he died of a heart attack and associated trauma resulting from his encounter with police.

Apparently, para-medics, called to the scene, administered a sedative they should not have given him. This is the callousness and disregard for Black Lives, from slavery days, psychologically painted and tainted as devoid of humanity, arising from the constructed American system with inherent racial bias in **Black Codes**, offering license to unleash terror on Black men, free or slave. Such laws empowered the police to view the enslaved Black, considered chattel, an animal without the attributes of humanity, a long-standing mental construct, designed to justify treatment meted out in callous and brutish tactics. This insensitivity or heartlessness is what killed George Floyd, Eric Garner, Amaud Arbery, Breonna Taylor and so many other Blacks listed within. Much of this is rooted in Biblical lore practicing Christians profess. This cold-heartedness breeds the fear the Black man feels in public but more in encounter with the police, and generation after generation Black parents have had to warn their young about how to act in such and other occurrences.

In a unique turn of events, the brutishness of the unconscionable act that murdered George Floyd so inflamed human sensitivities, their sense of decency, their need to express empathy all within the philosophic construct of the fatherhood of god and the brotherhood of man, etc., concerned Americans – Black, Brown, White, etc., – took to the streets to express outrage against the long-practiced system that encourages the devastating psychological and

GET YOUR KNEE
OFF OUR NECKS

social maltreatment of Blacks evident from 1619 to 2020. That sense of brotherhood, humanity, is what encouraged similar protest across the globe in support of Black human beings under siege.

GET YOUR KNEE OFF OUR NECKS is a demand that examines reaction to George Floyd's death in "The Eulogy by Rev. Al Sharpton;" "Placard Signs" carried in protest demonstrations; People's "Comments on the Times," in response to White House effete leadership that yet, divides rather than unites the nation; some "Names of persons murdered by Police;" "Greetings to the Graduating Class of 2020;" "Reactions to the Murder of George Floyd;" and a number of "Articles" such as "Biden is not the Enemy," even "Obama for Biden," and "Ben, Bill and Don," equally "This Russian Thing," Olympus has indeed Fallen;" and "Rudy and the Art of the Con," etc., among others that discusses failed leadership on part of Donald Trump on many fronts and inappropriate behavior, obstruction of justice, on part of the Department of Justice under Bill Barr in time of Carona-Virus Pandemic and crisis of racism. These happenings are reinforced in photos depicting citizens in angry protest, carrying placards, that expressed outrage at the manner in which such unacceptable inhumane behavior is perpetrated in their names and thereby they demand change become the order of the day. Naturally, such demands underscore the oppressor's resistance to change in many guises though it reveals the world's

9

recognition and sympathy for fellow humanity suffering under the yoke of racial oppression, particularly noticeable in time of pandemic and racism, in an America so many admire, love and want to make as a better place; if indeed it is the last hope for humanity.

Get your Knee off Our Necks – Photo –

GET YOUR KNEE OFF OUR NECKS

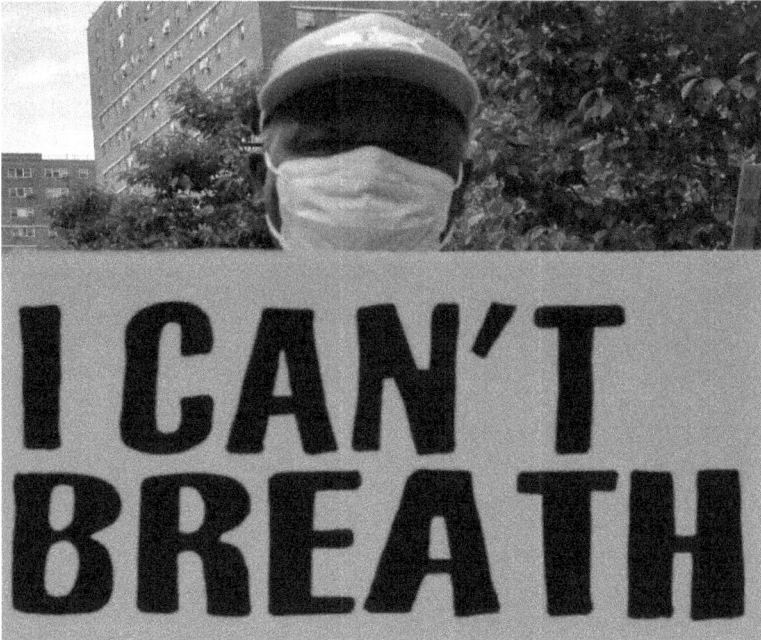

Get your Knee off Our Necks – Photo –

1."THERE'S NO RACISM BECAUSE BARACK OBAMA WAS ELECTED"

BY
DR. FRED MONDERSON

President Trump's senior Economic Advisor Larry Kudlow first argued, "There is no significant systemic racism in the police department" which has essentially been a talking point of senior administration officials such as Mr. O'Brien and

FREDERICK MONDERSON

Attorney General William Barr. Then Mr. Kudlow doubled down in a further asinine statement claiming, "There is no racism because the nation elected Barack Obama as President."

Get your Knee off Our Necks – Photo – George Floyd, the man whose murder forced the world to demand change in a time of pandemic and racism.

In response to a question on CNN's Erin Burnett's "Out Front" program, one Rapper, Jazzy, asked,

GET YOUR KNEE
OFF OUR NECKS

"Under which rock does Mr. Kudlow live?" If so, the two above statements would certainly indicate "Mr. Kudlow has come out!" Significantly, and time and time again, higher echelon persons, whether out of ignorance or otherwise, peddle a false narrative of both Coronavirus and racism in America. When challenged about racial disparity, inequality, injustice and how, in such a wealthy country, a significant proportion of the population lives in poverty and exists in conditions of housing squalor, are forced to make nutrition poor food choices and are victims of a lack of adequate health care, all resulting in a slew of diseases as diabetes, hypertension, high blood pressure, poor education, stroke and sub-standard housing which makes them especially vulnerable to viruses such as the flu and COVID-19, the Carona-virus Pandemic, then this issue becomes exacerbated.

Now, as the pandemic dramatically rises, the Trump Administration foolishly downplays the virus while escalating its lies, misinforming the public in this and many other areas in which his poor leadership has proved detrimental.

Given these prevailing conditions have made poor and Black citizens susceptible to the devastating ravages of virus and pandemic type challenges, police brutality should not be an added burden. It is certainly damaging psychologically and emotionally in a climate of fully conscious and unconscionable bias, as Wright Lassiter has exclaimed there is need

13

for a more significant response and, most important, "Corporate America has failed Black America through indifference, but especially because of good people staying silent when times are challenging." Therefore, when the Kudlows echo their ridiculous and falsely riddled diatribe; then they unfortunately, refuse to see or acknowledge their role, as the dominant element in the society that created the structure, systems and fundamentals of the contemporary malady, the problem becomes exacerbated.

Get your Knee off Our Necks – Photo –

Blacks are killed and discriminated against disproportionate to their numbers in the population. Thus, to deny racism exists flies in the face of reason and as such, those with power see no need for corrective action. Not that one rising tide lifts all

GET YOUR KNEE
OFF OUR NECKS

boats but that change will rob them of while privilege. However, it's not simply overt or covert racism, equally important is the potency of the issue of unconscionable bias. Take for example, the incident of a white woman confronting a black man bird-watching in Central Park, New York City. He filmed the whole incident of her being perhaps two dozen feet from him. Much more significant in the case of unconscionable bias, this individual knew the power of her claim, despite its falsity, that a Black man was assaulting a White woman. The police got there in record time. Its all part of the pathology of whatever while Black! That is, shopping while Black, sleeping in a dorm while Black, driving while Black, waiting for friends at Starbucks while Black, two young kids "Jay Walking" while Black, even "Bird-watching" while Black. There is no comparable "While white" challenge! Being Black in America should not be a death sentence or cause for alarm in the thoughts and actions of narrow-minded persons and especially in the actions of persons sworn to uphold and execute the laws to its full extent upholding the creed, "all men are created equal."

After Barack Hussein Obama was elected President in 2008, the then Mayor of Newark, New Jersey, Corey Booker was quoted, "The nation has now entered a post-racial era." Despite the challenges and circumstances in his state, Mr. Booker would go on to become a federal Senator in Congress. However, much transpired in the time from his

15

statement to today and thinking persons may come to the belief Mr. Booker must have finally realized the facts do not bear out his earlier simplistic and hurried, all be it, well intentioned assessment, then as now.

Get your Knee off Our Necks – Photo –

Afterall, concurrent with the "post-racial" statement, the "Birther falsity" was in full swing and thus made Mr. Booker seem out of touch, even as he was forced to recognize the significance of the orchestrated "Lynching of Barack Obama." As history has indicated, Donald Trump's rise to political prominence using "Birther" as a springboard garnered much support across the nation many thought a joke then, but actually such actions and similar behaviors foreshadowed his inner pathology. What is significant, all the foolishness and deadly encouragement Mr. Trump's guilty of, it's shameful, large as he is, he is only a microcosm of the malady he projects and represents. His racism is a manifestation of his base's ideology and mindset. Afterall, we're dealing with the South, home of the lynching states, slavery and confederate secession that resulted in untold deaths to preserve the Union. Add to this the 4004 lynchings the Equal Justice Initiative has been able to document from 1870 to 1950 and to this the "100 unsolved civil rights murders the FBI has files on. As we remember, from his declaring for the Presidency and descent on the elevator to deliver his "ban on Muslims" racist exhortation. This was an early warning of what would become a blow-up of Mr. Trump's distorted personality disorder. Nevertheless, while Trump's declaration would come later the first horse out of the gates was Senator Mitch McConnell whose blatant racist statement, "I intend to make Barack Obama a one term-President" was a wake-up-call warning to those who supported Mr. Obama and a call-to-arms for those who would certainly condone racist actions as well as those who stay silent in evidence of such wrong-doing. To this we may add the entire Republican Party who stood opposed to Mr. Obama earning the title, "Party of No!" This certainly must include the heavily armed Militias who continuously and publicly massed to "send a message" to Mr. Obama as they falsely championed the falsity, "Obama will take away your guns!" More important, Republican actions effectuated "to not give the Black guy a win," meant they blocked or

17

sabotaged every legislative agenda Mr. Obama proposed to the Congress despite the urgent need for such. When Mr. Obama's operation to eviscerate Osama bin-Laden reported its success, Many Republicans applauded by clapping with one hand! Still, Obama prevailed as a result of well-preparedness, a terrific work ethic, faith in the face of doubt, and unrelenting prayers by Black grandmothers that was an important ingredient in his successes in service to the American people.

GET YOUR KNEE
OFF OUR NECKS

Get your Knee off Our Necks – Photo –

Republican behavior towards President Obama, including what was later revealed of Mr. McConnell's actions as involved in the "plot" to undermine and sabotage the legally elected administration of the American government, call it treason, if you like, flies in the face of Edmund

Burke's dictum, "The only thing necessary for evil to triumph is for good men to do nothing." Given such, as President Obama anguished, crucified on the "Cross of Blackness," there appeared to be no good men, men of compassion, in the Republican Party who could but did not say any such behavior was wrong. This silence in face of unjust action and applauding Mr. Trump's divisive, deceitful and destructive behavior speaks volumes regarding not simply Mr. trump's behavior but also the mindset of those who support him with great fanfare. Afterall, the opposition against Mr. Obama was not simply in the legislative arena, but a climate of hate and disrespect sallied forth therefrom across the American landscape; so much so, the "lowest white man" projected his vile sentiments against a good and decent man, leading his nation out of an economic conundrum, social malaise and foreign policy debacle he inherited even as two wars raged that were consuming American lives. Strange, the economic and financial policies Obama put in place benefitted Donald Trump. Yet, the liar falsely claimed responsibility for gains in the economy and on Wall Street. Fact is, Senator Booker's "post racial" America had taken flight and hid, perhaps in company with Mr. Kudlow, under his rock.

GET YOUR KNEE
OFF OUR NECKS

Get your Knee off Our Necks – Photo –

Well, try as much as he did, President Obama's term came to an end and Number 45, Donald Trump, became his successor. Lo and behold, the "New penny" wore filthy underwear and within no time the new president began a litany of racist castigations of all, from Pope to Paul. Trump's actions were so devastating to the-for-long image of the American as a man of high moral ideals, religious conviction and upstanding acts of honor, truthfulness, integrity, compassion and courage the world so admired, but now in its passing such admiration has turned to scorn. These last few years of Trumping the nation has been saddened but also viewed with ridicule. Sadly, none of these high-standing qualities and more are possessed by the man who now occupies the White House. As if to reinforce the animosity and bad-will generated throughout his "Birther falsity" and foolishness and "full Monty" of Republican bad-faith acts and statements towards Mr. Obama, Donald Trump began rescinding every legislative, domestic and international constructive accomplishment the former President achieved in the interest of the American people. Be yond sad, not only s Donald Trump unrelenting in attempts to overturn Obamacare the Affordable Care Act (ACA), that provides Health Care for untold millions; he equally dismantled Obama's efforts to combat a projected pandemic that is presently raging as Covid-19 as far back as in 2014. Now, replaced both, trump offered not viable plans for either as more Americans are getting sick and dying Donald Trump expresses racist underbelly all against Barack Obama because he is Black. It seems this form of behavior is a continued effort of the "Don't give the Black Guy a Win" Republican mantra and strategy, all clothed in expensive yet filthy racist garb. And so, Mr. Trump withdrew from the Paris Climate Agreement, the PPT, the Iran Nuclear Deal and more. Trump even overturned Mr. Obama's regulations designed to curb polluting the air and water of the American environment. Even further, whereas the Affordable Care Act provided Health Care relief to untold millions, "Pied Piper" Trump and his Republican minions falsely dubbed this important health care legislation, Obamacare, and consistently have sought to wound and destroy its protections in the caustic "Don't give the Black Guy a win" maliciousness. Strange, that many in his base have benefitted from the Affordable Care Act though they don't like Obamacare.

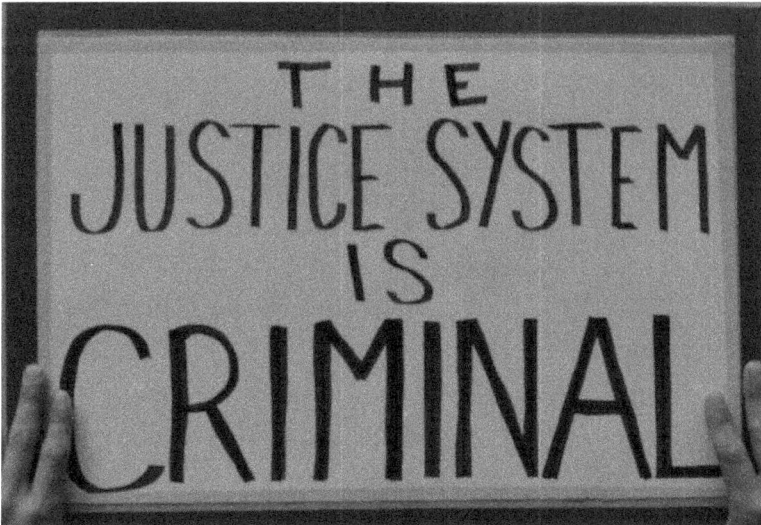

Get your Knee off Our Necks – Photo –

The interesting thing is, as Mr. Trump paraded his false piousness that his supporters never questioned, gradually the filth and odor of his dirty underwear began to come to light. Even in that glare of noon-day light, they failed to realize he had conned them into silence, now that his shadiness and potential criminality is boiling up to the surface; not only eggs, rotten fruit, coffee and more, stain their faces. Let's not forget, Trump told his followers, "Don't believe what you hear, don't believe what you read, don't believe what you see, that is not what's happening. Only believe what I tell you." Equally, he tells them, "We're managing the Carona-Virus," even as 130,000 Americans have died, 2 million infected, hospitals overwhelmed and the virus is spreading like wildfire among their locations, especially. Thus, he tells his base by implication, "Don't wear a mass and don't social distance" all among his many claims regarding the Corona-Virus and that we are now in a "Post-Covid-19-Virus era" despite the facts s how the Pandemic is now spreading like wildfire in the lands of his base!

Despite all of this, Republicans are still unable to grasp how deep they are in that "hole" the con man has absconded into with the riches he garners from playing president. Show us the taxes! Thus, we can't know whether the claim of his riches is genuine or more important, his economic entanglements across the globe, or whether he is indebted to the hilt, especially given the number of times he has filed for bankruptcy. A trademark of bombast, arrogance and filthy disposition allowed Donald Trump to not only daily chastise former President Obama, but quickly he racked up a super important mountain of lies and false or misleading statements that forces many to believe everything he tells is a lie, for such disbelief comes from being a liar. Like the monarch in Danny Kaye's children's song, "The King's New Clothes," Republicans ignored the rising flood-waters of his unbelievable amount of lies and misconduct as they became engrossed choosing to "See no evil, hear no evil, speak no evil" regarding Mr. Trump's egregious behavior. After a resounding batting record of more than twenty thousand lies, it was former Presidential Chief of Staff, General Colin

GET YOUR KNEE
OFF OUR NECKS

Powell who, interviewed on State of the Union, simply stated to the world, regarding President Trump, "**HE LIES!**"

Get your Knee off Our Necks – Photo –

FREDERICK MONDERSON

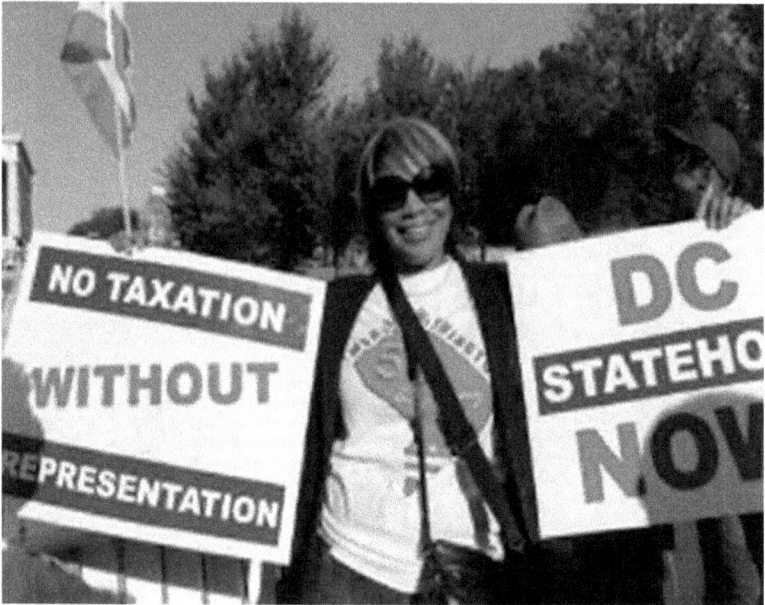

Get your Knee off Our Necks – Photo –

Today the nation is gripped by a tumultuous outpouring of protest against racist behavior, police brutality, glaring injustice, criminal and otherwise, unconscious bias, and the lack of empathy and insensitivity of a president whose entire tenure has been to encourage the most unconscionable behavior by the most unpleasant persons in the American mix. Persons such as the KKK, Nazis, Alt-right, flea-bags who would remain in the dark regions in which they festered for long, have now come out in the light of day to champion their man. As Governor DeSantis' opponent Mr. Gillam in Florida simply stated, "I'm not saying he is a racist, the racists say he is a racist" by their embrace of him. Donald Trump may contradictorily spout, "I am the most least racist person in the whole world,"

GET YOUR KNEE
OFF OUR NECKS

but the racist embrace him! Some, such as the virulent racist Ted Nugent and others including Sarah Palin were and are being entertained in the American people's White House. Couple this with the current Carona-virus Pandemic wreaking havoc on the American populace and that segment of the population suffering from the insufficiencies described above who became the most affected segment of the citizenry, is more than cause for alarm. Yet, rather than articulate unity, Trump's Carona-Virus strategy is to stroke culture wars and defend Confederate statues to his base. It's unfortunate that the 35 percent who see no evil in Trump's actions, do not see in embracing him as they do, they're exposing their own racist attitudes and beliefs.

Not altogether strange, but in Mr. Trump's initial declaration for the Presidency he discriminated against Muslims and immigrants, who today are in demonstrably significant numbers of front-line first-responders battling the Coronavirus. Trump also vented against Black elected officials and disrespected Black women in general, purportedly believing his excretion does not stink, his golden toilet, notwithstanding. Much of this, underscores his racist proclivities from refusal to rent to Blacks, don't want Black men counting his money, and the "Lu Lu," his rant against the "Central Park Five" now deemed the "Exonerated Five." Yet, in the beginning, he was given a pass hoping the office would remake the man! How sad today, as the

27

nation withers under the pandemic that has claimed more than one hundred and thirty thousand victims, some of which could have been avoided if Mr. Trump had demonstrated sound leadership by paying proper attention in the early expanding pandemic. As stated, the irony is that we notice, by their names, many of the specialists, doctors, front-line people, are the same ones he vilified to climb to his throne of falsity. Again, much of the victims of racism who exist at the bottom level of society and must work at menial and lifesaving jobs, are the ones most victimized in the racism and pandemic that today engulfs the nation.

Then George Floyd was murdered and the unconscionable nature of this act caused a tremendous beam of light to shine upon the darkness perpetrated in a system of bankrupt and effete leadership, cronyism that encouraged racist posturing and demonstrated display, Republican silence and evangelical complicity forcing the American people to take to the streets in organized and orchestrated protest. The murder of George Floyd is not an isolated incident for Black men have been killed by police brutality for centuries. Even some past killings are being resurrected and reexamined showing possibly police complicity in those deaths. More important, as the bodies began stacking up, people began to pay more attention to a malady of racism and racial discrimination that has come to characterize American indifference especially under Republican malfeasance.

GET YOUR KNEE
OFF OUR NECKS

Get your Knee off Our Necks – Photo –

The demonstrations have focused on what they term to be police brutality, misconduct and the pervasiveness of systemic racism. Now, even though Republicans deny racism exists, under challenges, their leadership scrambles to find solutions to the raging citizen discontent casting a negative light on the American character, all while the world watches and wonders. Nevertheless, Republican "paper-tiger" response amounts to nothing more than band-aid on lacerated wounds.

Now add this to the new revelations of the John Bolton's tell-all new book that claims "Mr. Trump is unfit to be President," he is consumed with being reelected, he seems a toy in the palm of Putin and Xi, while Kim has "played him like a fiddle."

FREDERICK MONDERSON

Further and emotionally devastating, Mr. Trump's niece's soon to be released book, the Trump family is trying hard to suppress, purportedly tells how he mistreated his own father, mocked his Alzheimer illness and displayed an inhumanity that is no longer alarming; but if, his father, then who is immune from his sinister and callus behavior? Who knows, "The glass episode," may signal the coming of his own malady.

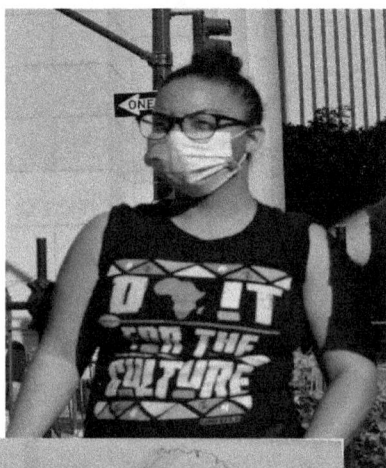

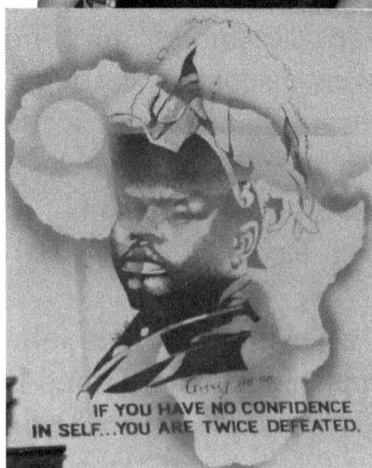

IF YOU HAVE NO CONFIDENCE IN SELF...YOU ARE TWICE DEFEATED.

Get your Knee off Our Necks – Photo –

GET YOUR KNEE
OFF OUR NECKS

The message is clear! "Do it for the future." "If you have no confidence in self ... You are twice defeated."

Now, in light of all this, we ask where are the Trey Gowdys and the McConnells, the "Stupid" Grassleys and so many others, especially the Representative Jordans, all stuck-on Donald Trump's "Ship of Fools" as they sail on into the "shit hole" environment he created that so stains their history in support of a man lacking empathy, a liar, one who subsumes the public good for his narrow self-interest, all betraying the expectations of the American people he was elected to serve.

Get your Knee off Our Necks – Photo –

No less significant, rather that unite the nation, recognize racism is a problem and offer solutions to

31

rectify long practiced behaviors demonstrated in harassment, arrests, high unemployment, death at the hands of police, destruction of black manhood that leads to self-hatred and black on black crime that in turn created a climate to blame the victim, and as the nation's leader, Mr. Trump is in denial of so much and more. He is more concerned about protecting statues of racist oppression that saving American lives. This is the man who want to be reelected for four more years! Sad!

Get your Knee off Our Necks – Photo – Sandra Bland (left) and Breonna Taylor (right).

2.   THE EULOGY
BY REV. AL SHARPTON
EPHESIANS 6: 10-20 –
THE FIGHT AGAINST EVIL

GET YOUR KNEE
OFF OUR NECKS

"Finally, let the mighty strength of the Lord make you strong. Put on all the armor that God gives, so you can defend yourself against the devil's tricks. We are not fighting against humans. We are fighting against forces and authorities and against rulers of darkness and powers in the spiritual world.

So, put on all the armor that God gives. Then when that evil day comes, we will be able to defend ourself. And when the battle is over, you will still be standing firm.

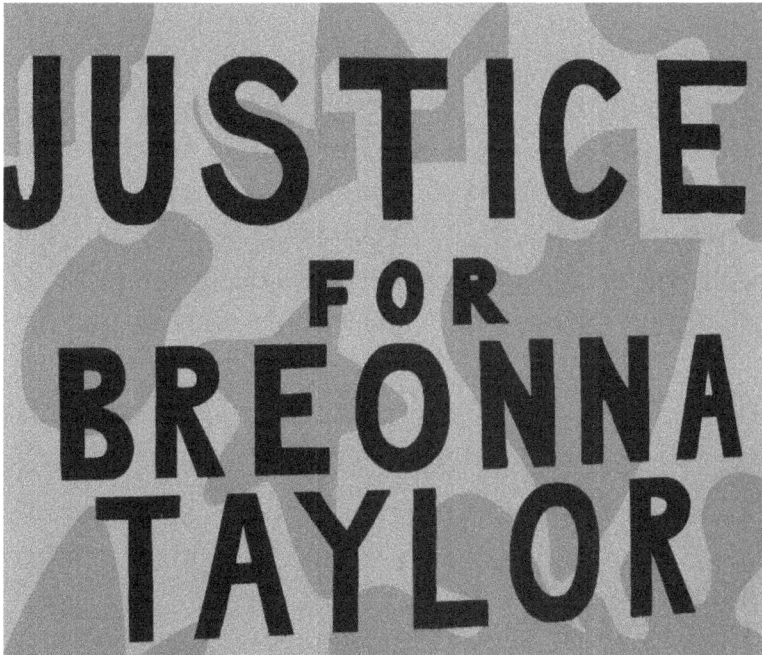

Get your Knee off Our Necks – Photo –
"Justice for Breonna Taylor."

FREDERICK MONDERSON

Be ready! Let the truth be like a belt around your waist, and let God's justice protect you like armor. Your desire to tell the good news about peace should be like shoes on your feet. Let faith be like a shield, and you will be able to stop all the flaming arrows of the evil one. Let God's saving power be like a helmet, and for a sword use God's message that comes from the Spirit.

Never stop praying, especially for others. Always pray be the power of the Spirit. Stay alert and keep praying for God's people. Pray that I will be given the message to speak and that I may fearlessly explain the mystery about the good news. I was sent to do this work, and that's the reason I'm in jail. So, pray that I will be brave and will speak as I should."

The following are remarks by **Rev. Al Sharpton** at the **Funeral of George Floyd** on June 9, 2020. Naturally, Rev. Al speaks faster than I can write, still I have tried to capture as much of his remarks as I could.

GET YOUR KNEE
OFF OUR NECKS

Get your Knee off Our Necks – Photo –

"These families came to stand with this family because they all went through this tragedy. Tyler Perry, Robert Smith, Floyd Mayweather, Jamie Foxx, Al. B. Shore.

Paul's letter to the Ephesians, **Ephesians** - encouraging we "be strong in the Lord."

"They will try to do everything to delay this trial. To wear down this family. Somebody must pay the cost for taking these lives.

"This is an intelligence that cannot be neglected.

"The same price for a Black Life is the same price for White life.

FREDERICK MONDERSON

Get your Knee off Our Necks – Photo –

"We will be here for the long haul. When the TV cameras are gone, we will still be here.

"In the audience we have Sabrina Fulton, Mother of Trayvon Martin; Gwen Carr, Mother of Eric Garner. Let's not forget Pamela Turner, Michael Brown, Ahmad Arbery.

"We are fighting an institution permitted with racism and wickedness in high places. It is full of venom. Full of something that motivates you.

"Until the law is upheld and they know they will go to jail, they will continue with the despicable behavior. They are protected by wickedness in high places.

GET YOUR KNEE
OFF OUR NECKS

"The signals they are sending, if you're in Law Enforcement, the law does not apply to you. If you break the law you should pay but you should know better.

"Such actions minimize Black Lives.

"Don't apologize. Give Colin Kaepernick his job back.

"Colin took a knee for families in this building and we don't want an apology, we want him to get paid.

"We want equal laws.

"How far we have to go to get justice?

"My great, grand-father was a slave in South Carolina. He was owned by someone named Sharpton. I went to the cemetery and saw a number of people named Sharpton. I realize they were all owned by a slave owner named Sharpton.

FREDERICK MONDERSON

Get your Knee off Our Necks – Photo –

"Every time I write my name, I'm writing our history. I am not signing my name; I'm signing someone else's name. A slave owner.

"The Lord said, 'I will pour out my spirit among all flesh.

"The grand children of slave masters tear down slave masters' statues in London and threw them in the river.

"God took the rejected stone. A job, position.

"God took the rejected stone and made him the corner stone.

GET YOUR KNEE
OFF OUR NECKS

"If you devalue one of us, you will realize he is of value to all of us.

"Genesis II – God formed man, He breathed life into him. Breathe came from god.

"Breath came from God. Breath sanctified from God. Breath is sacred.

Get your Knee off Our Necks – Photo –

"They are figuring out how to stop the protest.

"What we are dealing with is wickedness in high places.
"We were smarter than the underfunded schools you put us in. But you had your knee on our neck. We could run corporations and not hustle in the streets, but you had your knee on our neck. We had creative skills; we could do whatever anybody else

could do. But we couldn't, get your knee off our neck.

"Wickedness in High Places.

"Too many of you have been Trayvon Martin.

"We see the Police Union on one side. Righteousness on the other side. We have the vote. God is on our side.

"We have survived chattel slavery, Jim Crow, lynching, the Civil Rights Era. But god is still on the throne.

"The neck they sat on belonged to god's son.

"It's time to stand up and say, 'Get your knee off our necks.'

"Be not dismayed. God will take care of you. He may not be there with you but he is always on time.

"The lord will make a way. He walks with me, He talks with me, He tells me I'm his own.

"He provides the hungry with food and water. He is a sword and shield.

"The Lilly of the Valley.

"Be the morning star.

GET YOUR KNEE
OFF OUR NECKS

"He woke me up.

"The first shall be last and the last shall be first.

"Justice for George Floyd.

"Justice for Eric Garner.

"God will never leave us. The fight will go on.

"George Floyd, you touched the world.

"We won't rest until we get justice.

"He fought the good fight. He finished the race. He kept the fate.

"It is time to lay George Floyd down.

"Go get your rest! We will fight on!"

FREDERICK MONDERSON

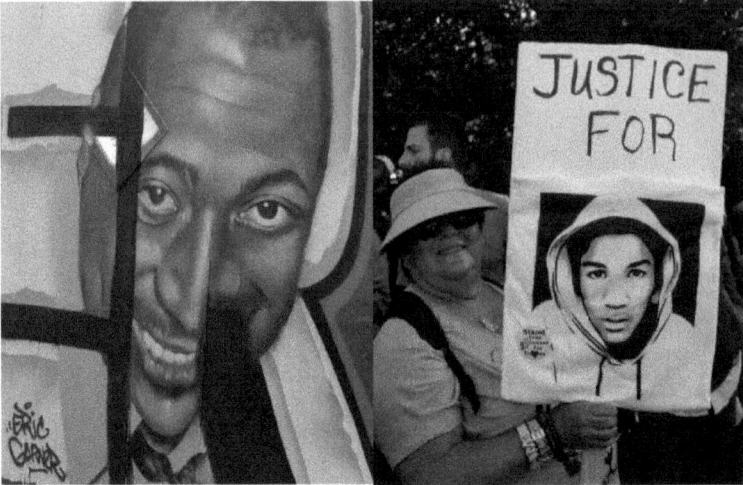

Get your Knee off Our Necks – Photo –
Eric Garner (left) and Trayvon Martin (right).

Get your Knee off Our Necks – Photo –
Sonny Carson (center) and Dr. Jack Felder (right), revered ancestors in Ghana accompanying the "Bones of Samuel Carson" alongside a young Brother accompanying them on the historic trip to open the "Door of Return."

3. THE DONALD TRUMP CONTRADICTION BY DR. FRED MONDERSON

President Donald Trump is faced with and is himself a contradiction, a conundrum, given he has created, in sports parlance, such are "unforced errors." That is to say, Mr. Trump and his "base" collectively act like a horde of lemmings confronting a cliff and sadly, not one of them is concerned to inform him of the impending danger. In his case, the danger is the loss of his most cherished ideal, to be re-elected as President. Perhaps that's why he urgently seeks the opening of the economy, praising new numbers on hiring, and Wall Street behavior. However, let's not forget, Mr. Trump promised to release his tax returns after the audit, which hides his, perhaps, false claims as to how many billions he owns. The fact is, perhaps his business is hurting and he hopes to turn around possible loses in his Corporation. Given he seems more concerned about money in his pocket, than equality and justice for a great many of the American people, one has to be naive to believe the Trump family is not benefitting from his presidency. Thus, after swilling at the public trough, Mr. Trump will finally be able to say, 'My 10 billion' was not exaggeration.

FREDERICK MONDERSON

All this notwithstanding, every time Mr. Trump opens his mouth the chasm widens because he is at war with the truth, and this makes it difficult for him to see the problems he creates. To emphasize this reality, we need to list some of the more visible issues that contribute to the contradiction and as they mount, we notice the conundrum or chasm he seems to fall into. In his case, however, its not despite what he and his followers think, its not the exotic fragrance they think they are smelling but what others see as the odor of that offensive place he so often relishes in.

Get your Knee off Our Necks – Photo –

The first contradiction facing Mr. Trump is, when he awakens and doing the bathroom routine, as he looks in the mirror, the reflection is not of Donald Trump but former President Barack Obama. Psychologists, even psychiatrists may use all

GET YOUR KNEE
OFF OUR NECKS

manner of language to describe this derangement but it is nonetheless real. The obsession with Mr. Obama is deep-seated and is more real than he or others think, for it is racial animosity in its most racist manifestation. While Mr. Trump's antiblack pathology is longstanding, his hatred of Mr. Obama is rooted in the psychological foundation of the Black image which fueled the "Birther" falsity with the unusual intensity girded in showmanship and con artistry. However, while Mr. Trump experiences these well-controlled maladies, Barack Obama's life goes on smooth as silk. In fact, while he does not get pay for it nor does he command an administration, great swaths of the American people, particularly the young, want to believe Mr. Obama is really the leader the nation needs at this time. This is a pain that burns inside Mr. Trump.

Get your Knee off Our Necks – Photo –

1.   Mr. Trump is a "pathological liar." We know he is in the "twenties," perhaps fast approaching 25,000 lies, false or misstatements and sadly, he does not know or acknowledges he has said such unbelievably wrong things. Perhaps, he does not

45

care, for in the final analysis, con men cannot retract the con, especially the long con. They have to go on and on and in the process end up wrapping themselves in lies similarly as the mummy wraps himself in untold lengths of cotton cloth. The Cretan reminded, "All Cretans are liars" and though Mr. Trump is not Cretan but American, his record of untruths forces others, right thinking persons, to disbelieve everything he says. Meaning, this is serious, for if Mr. Trump is telling the truth, because of his record, people have to believe he is telling a lie. In some circles, obfuscation labels these as "White lies." In Mr. trump case, its simply a mountain of white lies, approaching some nearly 25,000 false statements.

Get your Knee off Our Necks – Photo –

GET YOUR KNEE
OFF OUR NECKS

2.   Mr. Trump has been accused of and demonstrated racist behaviors and tendencies. We know in 1973 the Federal Government accused Mr. Trump of racial discrimination in his real estate practice because he refused to rent to Black people. Yet, the scuttlebutt is, thereafter "Young Donald" was making the rounds in Black circles to appear "Hip" and gain acceptance among the "cool cats of that age."   Nevertheless, his "Greatest Hit" was demonstrated in the case of the "Central Park Five" in which five young Harlemites were accused of ravishing a young white woman in Central Park. This incident was very traumatic for the City of New York and Mr. Trump threw gasoline in his defense of a young white woman's virtue. He was mum on the police murder of Breonna Taylor. The young men suffered tremendously; the painted picture cast a tremendously negative cloud on the image of Black men across the globe. Years later, it was proved, they were falsely accused for a young Hispanic man confessed to the crime. As usual in such cases, the City of New York sought to make restitution by compensating those now deemed, "The Exonerated Five." That ox of a man refused to accept their innocence and compensation.   This watershed realization underscored the reality of Mr. Trump's alternative reality. It sorts of scores with his advisor Kellyanne Conway, who explained Mr. Trump's use of "alternative facts" as he wallows in his "alternative universe."

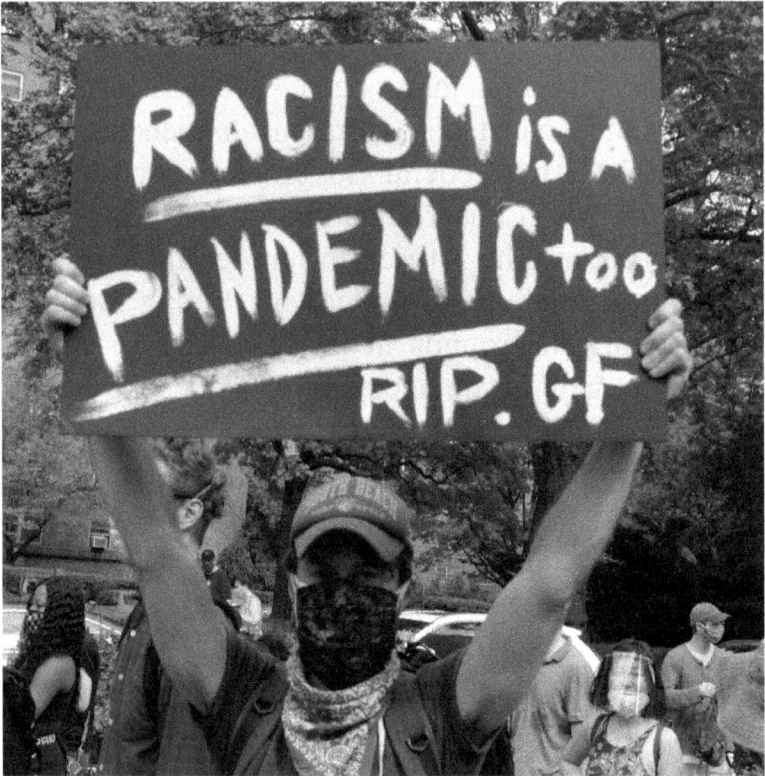

Get your Knee off Our Necks – Photo –

3.   Sadly, and no less significant, Mr. Trump kept turning out additional "Hits" by insulting Black leaders especially, Congresswoman Maxine Walters, three female Black reporters, that Johnson woman whose soldier husband died in a Special Operations mission in West Africa, and the four Black female House of Representative members whom he told "Go back from where you came." He won't say that to someone from Denmark. He insulted Rep. Elijah Cummings and the City of Baltimore, stating they represented "rat infested neighborhoods." He disrespected the NFL player

GET YOUR KNEE
OFF OUR NECKS

Colin Kaepernick who "took a knee" during the playing of the National Anthem to protest police killing of black men and the police brutality in general. Mr. Trump referred to those who "took a knee" as "Son of Bitches." What was not lost was the dreadful animosity of his facial expression when he barked, "You're fired."

Get your Knee off Our Necks – Photo –

4.   Again, the great obfuscator accused President Obama of being "incompetent" as a leader. Today, especially in light of the revolt spreading across the country, young people especially look to Mr. Obama as President and Donald Trump as a clown with dictatorial aspirations and himself incompetent as a leader. Even as Mr. Obama's rating as an ex-president is extremely high; yet, a slew of high-ranking retired Generals accused Mr. Trump of

undermining the Constitution through lack of leadership skills, insults across the board, his high-handed mentality and his belief he can do anything as a man above the law. He may not be but others are counting the days he has remaining at 1600 Pennsylvania Avenue, Washington, DC.

5.	As the head of his Republican political party, Mr. Trump uses threats and intimidation to keep his members in line. If they simply fart without his permission, he threatens to have their reelection challenged by another who would kiss his ring. In view of contemporary developments and that the generals have voiced their concerns, accusing Mr. Trump of dividing the nation, trampling upon the Constitution, they object to his lies, threats and ineffectiveness as a leader; the Republican Senator from Alaska, Makowski announced she is rethinking her support for Mr. Trump in the 2020 election. Instantly Trump responded, he will find a more amenable person to run against her when her term expires in 2022. Such a view not only demonstrates the vindictiveness of the man but clearly shows his arrogance, not only hoping but believing he will be in office in 2022 which means he will be re-elected by the American people. That element of the American population he calls his base and who thinks of him as golden will be in for a great surprise to realize he is actually costume jewelry painted gold. As a "thrower under the bus," he will so dispose of his base when it serves his purpose as when he feeds them false information about the virus and refuses to provide guidance of something as simple as wearing a mask.

6.   Donald Trump constantly tweets and retweets false, disparaging and racist mimes, some affirming white supremacy ideology, as "father of the nation" he should not do.

7.   Mr. Trump displays selective amnesia when he says things, then retracts, without acknowledging he said it and that it is wrong. More important, once one of his associates gets in hot water or says something that criticizes him, he claims "I hardly know the person" or disparagingly seeks to demean such persons.

Case in point. When George Papadopoulos was "caught up" in the Mueller Investigation, Mr. Trump and his cohorts claimed he hardly knew the man, despite a photo showing Papadopoulos two seats apart from Trump in a strategy session with him posing as a foreign policy expert. Then Papadopoulos was called simply a "water-boy." The same denial, call it, according to Dr. Leonard James, "The Petrine Syndrome" was exhibited, wherein his campaign manager Paul Manafort was also caught up in the "Russian thing," Trump said, "He was a campaign manager for just a few months." Those few months were crucial, however, for they encompassed the period of the Republican National Convention when the "Platform Plank" relating to removal of sanctions against Russia was effected or changed. So, Mr. Trump denied Manafort's influence but when charged and he initially refused to cooperate, to "Rat" on Trump, the President praised him by dangling a pardon. However, when Manafort realized how deep the hole he had dug, he changed his tune.

Get your Knee off Our Necks – Photo –

8.   The men who were part of Mr. Trump's inner circle, General Kelly, General McMaster and General Mattis who, out of disgust, chose to resign or depart, were then accused of all manner of things as ineffective in their responsibilities. Case in point at this juncture, the Marine General Mattis recently exposed Mr. Trump for the fraud that he is and pointed out how he is trying to divide America and trampling on the Constitution. In response, Mr. Trump attacked the General as "not being able to deliver" and so he fired him. Imagine, a lifetime of

military service, ending as a 4-star Marine General, compared to a bone-spur draft-dodger and the bad mouth. How sad, that General Kelly, even former Defense Secretary William Cohen extolled General Mattis not only as a good guy but one of the most decorated soldiers in American history. Those with insights such as General Kelly pointed out, General Mattis resigned because he could no longer stand the malarkey coming out of Door Number One, Door Number Two and Door Number Three in the Trump stall.

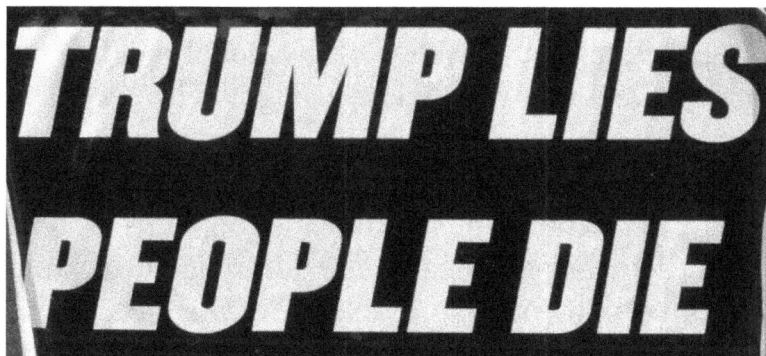

Get your Knee off Our Necks – Photo –

9.   Mr. Trump is not a good leader. He refuses to recognize, as a human being, perhaps he is not really, that mistakes can be made. It takes a big man to apologize. Then again, Mr. Trump is only obesely overweight but still a "little man" who wants to claim he is a "wartime commander" though he never has had military experience and more people died from the Coronavirus Pandemic on his watch,

130,000 than did in the Vietnam War 55,000, he dodged claiming "bone spurs."

10.   Mr. Trump is a master of misrepresentation. So much so, he was once clocked at more than twenty thousand false or misleading statements though he equally likes to take credit for the good but disowns the bad. What a character! Now he wants to be and is trying to be reelected in November despite his dismal record and ineptitude as a leader at a time when America is in crisis from Carona-virus and racism and he doubles down on culture wars and con federate flags. The president does not realize, though he is banking on the economy turning around rapidly, a Wall Street upsurge, unemployment numbers dropping, etc., that the American people who are forgiving to a fault, will give him four more years, even as he appeals not to the "Better angels" of America, but the "worse devils" of its dark side.

If so, will we end up with 40,000 lies and 200,000 Pandemic deaths. But this will not be given the people are Trump fatigued through lies, racist division in culture wars, ineffective leadership and overall disrespecting the Office of the Presidency.

GET YOUR KNEE OFF OUR NECKS

Get your Knee off Our Necks – Photo –

4. THE WORLD IS LAUGHING AT

AMERICA – NO!
BY
DR. FRED MONDERSON

No, Mr. President, the world is not laughing but languishing and lamenting in solidarity with the oppressed in your country. They are not laughing. They are weeping and protesting that **BLACK LIVES MATTER**, everywhere, though it's under assault under your tenure as President for 35% of Americans.

In his attempt to rebuke particularly states with democratic governors s het current popular protests in challenge to systemic racism and death of George Floyd, President Trump declared "The World is Laughing at America" because governors refused to ignore the deadly pandemic by recommending masks, social distancing, and other preventative measures. As a pathological liar Trump wants the American people to believe whatever he says, no matter how outlandish. Yet, Mr. Trump has failed miserably to convince right thinking Americans of anything meaningful as his presidency has unfolded in nearly four years.

Mr. Trump has claimed to be a "Wartime President;" yet, over these four years he has sought to engage the "enemy" on a myriad of fronts. Classic military strategy dictates commanders avoid fighting on two or more fronts and the best example is, Adolf Hitler in World War II caught between the Western Alliance and Russia. Mr. Trump, like the "absolute fool" as Joe Biden calls him, has picked fights with practically everyone on the planet. That is, except his idol, America's gravest enemy, Vladimir Putin to whom he gave the store.

Perhaps, in his confused state, given he commands the world's mightiest military Trump thinks he could do anything to anyone and have its backing. So, he insulted 70 percent of the American populace, then America's strongest allies and more. Of note, he has not insulted Vladimir Putin, the Russian strongman nor even President Xi of China and Kim who got the better of him.

In reflection, his base wanted to award him a Noble Prize, to this day, he can't comprehend Kim was "a bridge too far." He has certainly earned the "Give

GET YOUR KNEE
OFF OUR NECKS

away the store in chief title, for eh gave away the store to Kim Jung Un, to Vladimir Putin, to President Xi and unfortunately this "mark" does not realize they picked his pocket.

Get your Knee off Our Necks – Photo –

Some years ago, the newsmagazine *Newsweek* ran a cover entitled, "Why are Obama's critics of dumb."

As a representative of the 35 percent of the American populace, Mr. Trump's "Base," he had convinced them, the foul air he exudes does not blow in their direction. Some may have seen a commercial of two men standing in a large vat of beverage and the older of the two asks the young man, "Why did you put sugar in the mix?" The younger man responded to the listening audience, saying essentially, "Only drink the beverage in front of me, not that at my rear."

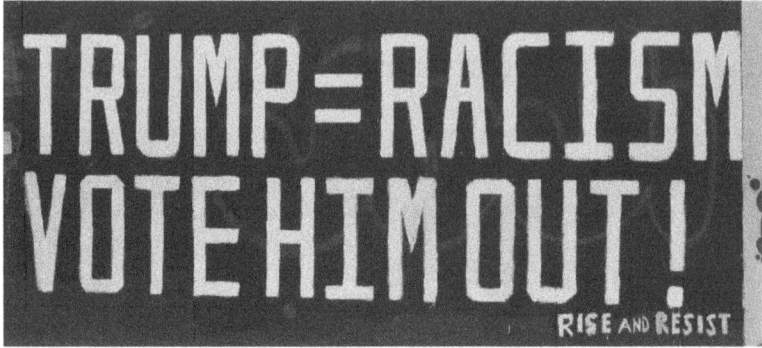

Get your Knee off Our Necks – Photo –

Again, it's like dr. Ben Carson, who emerged as the poster face of the Heritage Foundation as he criticized the Affordable Care Act misnomered "Obamacare" as "worse than slavery." Thinking individuals could envision as Dr. Carson delivered his diatribe and amid the responsive congratulatory accolades lavished on his eloquence, he may have convinced himself, he sailed a boat different from Mr. Obama and his supporters. Perhaps one person in his audience, in congratulating the orator would have exhorted, "The Nigger Doctor has spoken." Sadly, and again, perhaps as Malcolm X reminded, "You're not discriminated against because you're a Mason or an Elk, you're catching hell because you're black!" Unfortunately, and thanks to the 30 pieces of silver or chitlings that fell from the master's table, as approbation Dr. Carson refuses to see himself associated with the negroes in Obama's boat. Even further, Dr. Carson and other Trump sycophants, black ones especially, are unable to see the beam in his eye and do not have the gumption like the weasel in the movie **Zootopia** who reminded his cohort, "Its DNA not dinner" and lost as he was responded, "I know what I'm saying" in his delusionary state.

For his part, Mr. Trump has delusionary memory, selective amnesia, for he seems to have forgotten his United Nations' encounter. In that address wherein he walked into the Hall holding his lapels with both hands and in a shuddering tone, said, "I will destroy North Korea." Vain as he is, he fell for Kin's charm and like a "dumb bell," "fell in love." Well played, Kim got what he wanted, world stage recognition and he left Donald Trump at the altar. In the next encounter, the entire body began laughing and the tricky con man that he is, Mr. Trump told his followers, "They're not laughing at me. They're laughing with me!" Afterall, he had earlier reminded them, "Don't believe what you read; don't believe what you hear; don't believe what you see; that's not happening. Believe me." Remember the commercial where the pitchman complains, "Some people think lactose is not real milk, so all these cows behind me must be big dogs." And, so Mr. Trump's followers believe him as they do believe the world is laughing at the governors' response to the protest in its many manifestations. For one thing, the world seems to have shown respect for Governor Andrew Cuomo who has demonstrated exemplar leadership especially in his response to the Carona-Virus Pandemic.

Get your Knee off Our Necks – Photo –

5.   GEORGE FLOYD

GET YOUR KNEE
OFF OUR NECKS

VAN JONES – George Floyd was a victim of "Sudden in Custody Death Syndrome."

LAURA COATES – "This is a disregard for human life. A reckless disregard for human life. Imagine, his hand in his pocket in the prone position."

REDDITT HUDSON – St. Louis Police Officer – "George Floyd was in deep distress."

ANONYMOUS – "Lock them up now. White supremacist members in that police force. Here we have an escalation of frustration."

"Police Officers are speaking out across the nation."

"The nation is deeply wounded."

DIONNE SEARCEY – THE NEW YORK TIMES – "In a service punctuated by gospel music, Mr. Floyd's relatives told personal stories of the man they knew as Perry, and whom people in the neighborhood had called 'Big Floyd.' He had a gift of making people feel welcome. His brother Philonise Floyd called him a 'general,' someone who always had a line of friends behind him."

"Everywhere you go and see people, how they cling to him. They wanted to be around him,' he said."

FREDERICK MONDERSON

Get your Knee off Our Necks – Photo –

"Being in the house with my brother, it was inspiring, he added, because my mom used to take in other kids, and they were George's friends."

"He recalled sharing a bed with his big brother. Together, they played football and ate banana-and-mayonnaise sandwiches and used an oven to dry their clothes."

"One of his cousins, Shareeduh Tate, said, 'The thing I miss most about him is his hugs. He was just this big giant."

GET YOUR KNEE
OFF OUR NECKS

Get your Knee off Our Necks – Photo –

6. COUNCILMEMBER ROBERT E. CORNEGY, JR.

Remarks: Vigil for Victims of Police Violence
June 9, 2020
Good morning.

Thanks to all those joining us today to honor the lives of those killed by police violence. Though we will say their names, each name stands for so much more.

Their names stand for a life. A life as a mother or father, wife or husband, daughter or son.

FREDERICK MONDERSON

Their names stand for family, friends, loved ones, and communities aching with grief.

Their names stand for countless more unnamed who were killed by the police.

And, to me, their names stand for a profound pledge at the end of Langston Hughes' poem "Let America Be America Again." Hughes writes:

O, yes,
I say it plain,
America never was America to me,
And yet I swear this oath—
America will be!

Out of the rack and ruin of our gangster death,

The rape and rot of graft, and stealth, and lies,

We, the people, must redeem

The land, the mines, the plants, the rivers.

The mountains and the endless plain—

All, all the stretch of these great green states—

And make America again!

GET YOUR KNEE OFF OUR NECKS

Get your Knee off Our Necks – Photo –

In the face of injustice – in the face of anguish and abuses, in the face "of the rack and ruin" – we are summoned to the true meaning of our values of freedom and liberty.

"America never was America to me; And yet I swear this oath – America will be!" It is an oath that, "We, the people, must redeem"

We redeem that oath by changing the narrative that led to these deaths. By gathering as we are today, as a community of many faiths, many ethnicities, and many backgrounds - and changing that narrative together.

We must advance legislation to hold police accountable, ban chokeholds, make police

FREDERICK MONDERSON

misconduct and corresponding discipline more transparent. We must pass 911 anti-discrimination and 911 anti-harassment legislation that makes false reporting and using 911 as a tool of intimidation to menace others a hate crime. We must work with community groups and the City's Office of Criminal Justice to establish anti-racism classes so that district attorneys and judges have even more tools to sentence those who make the 911 calls on the basis of "living while black" offenses - birdwatching, babysitting, waiting for a friend in Starbucks, or barbecuing. Legislation is one of the tools we have to change the narrative.

Even more important than legislation as a tool to change the narrative – our being together today. Our engagement, our uplifting our voices with one another.

Together we can change the narrative.

Thank you.

GET YOUR KNEE
OFF OUR NECKS

Get your Knee off Our Necks – Photo –

7. THE DEVIL'S CLOAKING
DEVICE
BY
DR. FRED MONDERSON

A constant problem confronting Captain James Kirk in the many Star Trek episodes was the Klingons using cloaking devices to sneak-up on that champion of truth and justice. The American way! As entertainment theater of that age demonstrated, truth and justice always triumphed over dishonesty and dirt. That is, after Captain Kirk had detected and defeated the adversaries, we saw the Klingon ships limp off and fade away into oblivion. Such, however, is difficult to achieve these days.

FREDERICK MONDERSON

In a movie with Keanu Reeves and Al Pacino, it has been said, "One of the biggest hoaxes the devil perpetrated is the belief that he does not exist.

President Donald Trump comes very close, if he has not yet done so, of perpetuating the classic above con game. Very often it is said of the blind man who acknowledge, "I see" while people with clear vision either do not or refuse to see what's before their very eyes and noses. In this, Mr. Trump has convinced his base, "Don't believe what you hear; don't believe what you read; don't believe what you see; That is not what's happening. Believe what I tell you." In that vein, Mr. Trump's base cannot accept the poll numbers; they cannot acknowledge the live-feed on Television; but they can believe the numbers on Wall Street and the unemployment figures, especially those reported this past week, all as the mat covered the dirt beneath.

GET YOUR KNEE
OFF OUR NECKS

Get your Knee off Our Necks – Photo –

Much of this brings us to the realization, not that Mr. Trump is the devil, which is a stretch but he has so fooled all observers, or so he thinks, the question then becomes is there a day of final reckoning. In America, the Constitution provides the basis of law and it guarantees citizens certain rights and privileges labeled the Bill of Rights. Among the many privileges the American system provides is the right to vote and for the office of the Presidency, it comes the first Tuesday in the month of November, every fourth year. This expression of the ballot is a cherished privilege Americans take seriously for they choose the best and the brightest who are selected to make laws that reflect their beliefs and cultural practices.

FREDERICK MONDERSON

As a registered voter and journalist, I was concerned about some issues in my community and wrote an article critical of the Governor George Pataki. The editor of my newspaper responded, "The governor is elected. We have to live with this. His term of office expires in a given time period and if you're not satisfied with the job he is doing, then when the election comes around, you can vote him out."

Its been said, "Politicians are concerned about two things. Getting elected and getting re-elected." Mr. Trump, the unexpected winner of the 2016 election to the Presidency came to the view he was the best thing for the American people. The "old style" television news personality Lou Dobbs voted Mr. Trump the Greatest American president ever." Naturally, this was a vote of one, for me. Many of the Presidents Mr. Trump was compared to faced problems, foreign and domestic during their tenure in office. In seeking to address each issue as they presented themselves, the Chief Executives sought the help and support of the great swath of the American populace for they understood the cliché, "Unity is Strength" and "United We Stand!" Perhaps Mr. Trump never believed this and he certainly did not seek to cultivate this potent element that strengthens leadership. He did a very good balancing act in catering to the "five percent" of wealthy Americans and the "thirty" percent of his base.

GET YOUR KNEE
OFF OUR NECKS

Get your Knee off Our Necks – Photo –

For the most part, while the "five percent" benefitted from the "nation's biggest tax cut" that did not truly bring the "supply side economic" gains it promised, Mr. Trump used his "Cloaking devise" to obscure the reality of the American situation and convinced the "thirty percent" who did not benefit from his tax give away, that opponents were to blame. Call it sleight of hand or sleight of tongue, but the great magician so cloaked the dinner table, his supporters walked away with empty plates and were happy, singing songs of praise despite their empty bellies.

FREDERICK MONDERSON

In old country folk-lore parlance the story is told of Brer Anansi, a great trickster, who like a vampire was not opposed to suck the blood of his family. Here's how he did it. There were seven of them. He had five children, a wife and himself. Times were hard but at a prepared dinner they had "six plantains.' With the table set, all seated, and having cooked their morsel, Mr. Anansi shared the six plantains to his family as all sat at table. Everyone was given a plantain except Mr. Anansi whose plate was empty as they set about to eat. Everyone turned to Papa Bear and noticing his plate was empty offered half a plantain. He ended up with three plantains and they each half of one.

This is not too different from Mr. Trump in his approach to the American populace in general. Beyond the "Birther" falsity, even though the American economy especially was well on its way to recovery through practices and policies put in place by the Obama administration, Mr. Trump touted the nation's good fortune when the stock market rose and unemployment fell, all at his doing. Even before that, egotistically braggadocio as he was, he exploited the mounting success after success Obama set in place. During the election of 2016, Mr. Trump broke with presidential tradition and refused to release his tax returns. Ostensively, he claimed he was being audited by the IRS and as soon as this was over, he would release his returns and Americans would see how rich, give and take, ten billion, he was "Really rich!" Well, that empty promise, like so many, came and went and he did not deliver, yet he accused the great American General Mattis of "not delivering."

As fate and destiny often intervenes, the Covid-19 Corona virus hit America with resounding devastation in terms of deaths and economic casualties. Added to the many unpresidential behaviors Mr. Trump displayed, insulting persons left, right, up and down, he even threatened the foundations of the American Constitution.

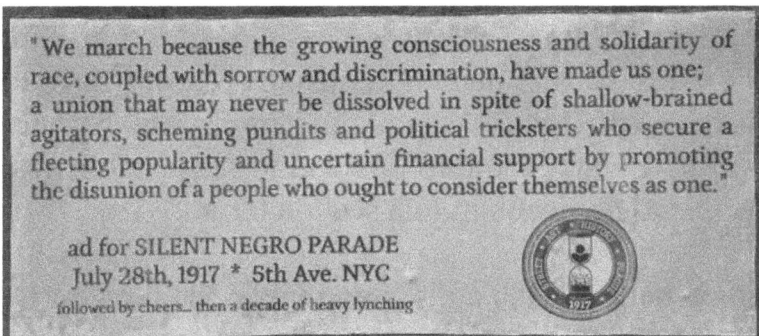

"We march because the growing consciousness and solidarity of race, coupled with sorrow and discrimination, have made us one; a union that may never be dissolved in spite of shallow-brained agitators, scheming pundits and political tricksters who secure a fleeting popularity and uncertain financial support by promoting the disunion of a people who ought to consider themselves as one."

ad for SILENT NEGRO PARADE
July 28th, 1917 * 5th Ave. NYC
followed by cheers... then a decade of heavy lynching

Get your Knee off Our Necks – Photo –

Mr. Trump is a pathological liar and employing his "Cloaking device" of meaningless chatter, he pushed very hard to open the American economy. Given the nation was hurting economically, many saw this as prudent thought, with the pandemic still raging, some still advised and practiced caution. He sent his lemmings to liberate Michigan especially and they came armed to the teeth to the State Capital building. Today, Michigan's Carona-virus numbers are up, perhaps the spread was a result of those liberation efforts by people prepared to die for Donald Trump. However, with Mr. Trump's record of untruths and ulterior motive practices, critical thinkers wondered if there was more to the president's care for the nation's economic well-being or his own bottom line. After all, not having released his tax returns, and having lost funds in the undulative nature of the stock market combined with the devastation of the pandemic that forced closure of much of the nation's businesses, one has to wonder whether the smoke and mirrors is to shore up Mr. Trump's bottom line and to further convince people to re-elect him to a second term.

Some believe such a disaster could open the door to some 40,000 lies and misstatements and perhaps more than 200,000 deaths from the Pandemic. If that happens, then the plague would have descended upon America and Mr. Trump would be considered, in Lou Dobbs prognostication, the greatest American president in the failed state category given his poor leadership, divisive nature and racist underbelly all wrapped in disgusting bombast.

GET YOUR KNEE OFF OUR NECKS

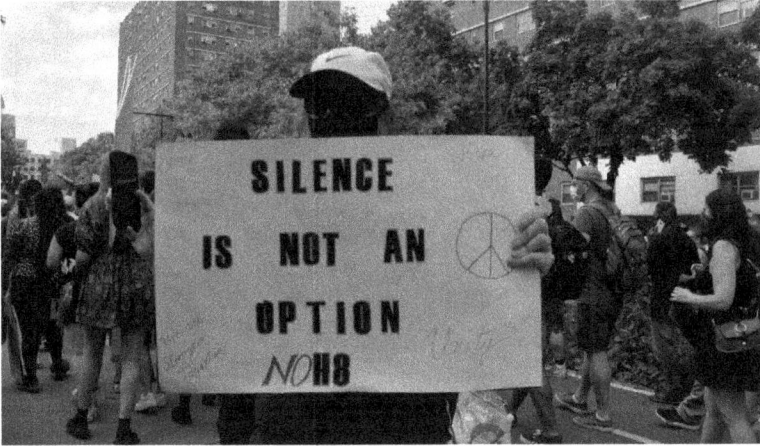

Get your Knee off Our Necks – Photo –

8. "BLACK MARTYRS AND THE AMERICAN IDEAL" BY DR. FRED MONDERSON

The events that gave rise to the American Revolution produced a number of important documents, viz., the **Declaration of Independence**, **Articles of Confederation** and the **Constitution**. In addition, there were shibboleths and actions that helped define and lay the grounds of what became the American personality and the ideal he has been aspiring to, a society of equality and justice for all. This is considered an attainment in an ongoing process, nearly two hundred and fifty years in the making. However, from the beginning, shibboleths as "Give me liberty or give me death," whose main proponent has been Patrick Henry; and the "Tree of Liberty" needs to be refreshed periodically proved galvanizing in time of revolutionary challenge. Yet still, actions that characterized such expressions lay the foundation and began the long journey of three centuries process of creating the more perfect union exemplified in the American ideal. Most important, this involves the shedding of blood, watering the "Tree of Liberty," the apotheosis in martyrdom to achieve the symbol, the shining star of what constitutes the essence of the American experience. Today, it is considered "Gold Star." However, his parents, never enjoyed the privilege and honor of having their son die in cause of America, becoming "Gold Star Parents."

The first and most authentic American hero, its first martyr, Crispus Attucks, was an African-American even though he did not enjoy the proclivities, of life, liberty and the pursuit of happiness of being American. After all, some 80 years later, in the *Dred Scott versus Sandford* (1857) case Chief Justice Roger, a defender of slavery, ruled essentially, blacks were "not American citizens and could not bring suit in federal courts." Even more long-lasting, according to Chief Justice Taney, the black man 'did not have any rights a white was bound to respect.' Naturally, the enslaved Black man was considered property, chattel and certainly, in social and psychological realities, color was an indicting factor. Beyond the great and enduring current

GET YOUR KNEE
OFF OUR NECKS

protests against police brutality today, we see the color question playing out where an African-American was threatened with calling the police on a Black man in Central Park as he "bird watched." They came because a big Black man was threatening a white woman. Thank goodness he was filming her some distance away. Let's not forget, the Smith woman, who drowned her two children and claimed, "A black man abducted them." They were later found, in a car-seat, in her car, in a lake and all because she wanted to have an affair with a white man and the children were in the way. Remember the one at the bank where the Black man wrote the name "Obama" on the skin of a white woman.

Today's protests following the murder go George Floyd decried such behaviors and mentality as part of America's original sin of slavery ad the system it created to consider the Black man as no more than property, 3/5 of a person, devoid of the humanity of whites and therefore any treatment, however, harsh is justified. As W.E.B. DuBois has written, "The system was designed in the beginning to fail the enslaved African in America."

FREDERICK MONDERSON

Get your Knee off Our Necks – Photo –

9. COMENTS ON THE TIMES/ VOICE OF THE PEOPLE

BARACK OBAMA – To the Graduating Class of 2020 – "I want you to know that you matter and you do."

REV. JERRY MCAFEE – "Reality of **GOD**!" "Possibilities of Relationships!"

DC MAYOR BOWSER – Donald Trump is "A man who is scared and alone."

GET YOUR KNEE
OFF OUR NECKS

JOE BIDEN – Donald Trump is - "An absolute fool."

BEN JEALOUS - "Donald Trump sinks to a new low." "He is despicable. He uses rubber bullets. His callousness is worse than flat."

REV. AL SHARPTON - "Get your knees off our backs."

GENERAL JOHN KELLY - "Trump did not fire Mattis as he claims."

MARTIN LUTHER KING III - "When we stood-up for 8 minutes and 46 seconds this was the most emotional moment in George Floyd's funeral memorial."

FREDERICK MONDERSON

JOHN HARWOOD - "Donald Trump is not governed by fixed principles. He demonstrates erratic behaviors and has a short attention span."

GENERAL KELLY - "Jim Mattis is an honorable man."

ANONYMOUS - "In Donald Trump we see images of fear. He is afraid of the American people."

FORMER DEFESE SECRETARY WILLIAM COHEN -
"We cannot sanction extra-judicial killings, murder, lynchings."

MARTIN LUTHER KING III - "People must be registered, mobilized, organized, assert and charged. There must be a change of consciousness. They must hold the Police Department accountable. This is not just a movement about Black people. People are raising their voices to say this is not enough. Donald Trump is not a great president. The Greatest presidents were Abraham Lincoln, Franklin D. Roosevelt and George Washington."

CARL BERNSTEIN - "A good leader must put the national interest ahead of self-interest. Donald trump has put his reelection above the people's interest. A cold civil war preexisted Donald Trump but the president exacerbated this. He has lost his

GET YOUR KNEE
OFF OUR NECKS

credibility from the beginning. He has disrespected people of color, immigrants, gone after political enemies. He does bear responsibility. He has been asleep at the switch."

TODD AXTELL, Police Officer, St. Paul, Minnesota – "We must all open our minds, our hearts as to what is happening in our country."

"Our hearts ache with what is going on in our country right now!"

"Police officers have an absolute duty to intervene when they see behavior not sanctioned."

Get your Knee off Our Necks – Photo –

BISHOP MIRIAM EDGAR BUDDE – "We of the Diocese of Washington, DC, distance ourselves from the words and actions of this president. We need moral leadership. We need political leadership. There is an abuse of the sacred symbols of the people of this nation. The president's behavior is antithetical to everything the people of this nation stands for. The president stood on sacred ground using the Bible for a political Photo Op but he did not pray. This is abuse of religious symbolism."

Get your Knee off Our Necks – Photo –

"Dr. King decried the silence and inaction of good people."

JON BATISTE -   "We're never alone. The ancestors are always with us."

GET YOUR KNEE
OFF OUR NECKS

"This is a catalyst moment to deal with issues and problems in our society."

Get your Knee off Our Necks – Photo –

CHERYL DORSEY – Detective, Retired, Los Angeles Police Department. "There is a place for Black Police Officers. They are the ones who would say, 'Hey man, don't do that.'"

"Los Angeles PD is predominantly Hispanic and there a problem with that. Police Unions are part of the problem. They do not want to do anything to deter the problem."

"The Buffalo police who resigned from the Emergency Response Department should have resigned from the Police Department."

Get your Knee off Our Necks – Photo –

GENERAL COLIN POWELL – Former Secretary of State and White House Chief of Staff – "I agree with Generals Mattis, Kelly and Allen."

"I am proud of what the protesters are doing. We are at a turning point."

"We have a Constitution and we must abide by it."

"The president lies and he gets away with it because Congress has nothing to say."

"I could not vote for him in 2016 and I can't vote for him in 2020. It started with the Birther Movement. He insulted Immigrants. I am the son of an Immigrant. He insulted John McCain. He has divided the country. I have been a friend of Joe

GET YOUR KNEE
OFF OUR NECKS

Biden for 40 tears. We have worked on social issues and I'm going to vote for him."

"The President should follow the Constitution."

Trump "abuses and demonizes the press, friends, democrats, Germans, the World Health Organization, the United Nations and much more. He has a disdain for American foreign policy. He acts without consultation with the Joint Chiefs. There are restraints on his power. His actions are dangerous for our country."

"He lies!"

Comments from **MARQISE FRANCIS OF YAHOO NEWS** Interview with Activist **DeRAY MCKESSON**

FREDERICK MONDERSON

Get your Knee off Our Necks – Photo –

DERAY MCKESSON: "We think this immediate crisis is around police violence, right? And acknowledgment that the police kill around 1,100 people each year, but the police have killed more people since the protests in 2014, not less. And then a third of all the people killed by strangers are actually killed by a police officer.

"Then with the backdrop of the presidential election coming up, most Black people are not fans of President Trump. But then a lot of people also aren't feeling former Vice President Joe Biden. So, is Joe Biden doing enough for Black Americans?"

"I think that's like a false-choice question. I think Trump is so egregious that it's, like, we might want something better from Biden, but Trump is just so wild."

"We never thought there'd be a president who would ban whole countries on Twitter. We never thought there'd be a president who would seek the death penalty for drug dealers, right? Are you even thinking about him with the protest? What does it look like? So, I think that that is so wild and bad that there's nothing Biden has done or could do that would make me think he wouldn't be a fit president up against this guy".

"Now, I think that Biden isn't as progressive as we want him to be. I think there's some pushes there. I also think that Biden's platform is actually better than Biden's ability to talk about that platform sometimes."

JAMELE HILL – *The Atlantic* – "Newsrooms do not reflect the community we cover and this reflects the attitudes in the country."

FREDERICK MONDERSON

Get your Knee off Our Necks – Photo –

KAREN ATTIAH – *The Washington Post* – "Most newsrooms are uniquely unprepared to cover what's happening across the country."

NICOLE HANNAH-JONES – *The New York Times* – The problem is, "Newsrooms don't want to be seen as diverse attempts to explain diversity and racial expressions in the community at large."

BRIAN SELTZER – *Reliable Sources* – "Sean Hannity is lying to the audience. This is misleading."

JAMELE HILL – Hannity is like "Asking a zebra to change his stripes."

GET YOUR KNEE

...ECKS

Get your Knee off Our Necks – Photo –

"**OUR JOB IS AGITATION**" The news reporting, that is!

JOURNALISTS CALLED IN SICK TO PROTEST PHILLY INQUIRER

NICOLE HANNAH JONES – Presentation of "The news is much better now." However, "76 percent of the population believe systemic racism is a problem."

KAREN ALLIAH – "The entire world is watching. I hope the people in power are listening."

KEITH ELLISON – "There has not been any single lawsuit against any single municipality since Donald Trump became president. He called them back.'

"People are trying to tarnish your protest. Don't let them do it. Protect your protest. Use your phones to take pictures of people looting, burning and breaking the law. Protect your lawful protest."

"One Team, One Goal, One Mission."

MICHAEL ERIC DYSON – Author of "Tears We cannot Stop" – "There is deeply entrenched irony and despair in this country."

"We live in the United States of Amnesia."

"It is like the Coronavirus – Something we cannot see."

"Whites are rioting too. They're rioting against the Blacks in the Corps, in the Police. They're rioting against the Blacks as do the far right."

GET YOUR KNEE
OFF OUR NECKS

Get your Knee off Our Necks – Photo –

DR. BEN CARSON – "Are there racists around, absolutely. They were there yesterday. They are here today. They will be around tomorrow."

"I don't generally go into demonizing other people."

The George Floyd episode was "Horrified to see. It was blatant and terrible murder."

KAREN BASS – Chairwoman of the Black Caucus. "This moment is incredibly inspiring in saying enough is enough."

"It is inspiring to get the Legislation we need."

"We're in a real moment in our country."

"The bill we are pushing, among other things seeks Police Accountability. There is no way to track officers' behaviors. They need training and accountability. Its only the people intervening by taking photos of misbehavior. The incident in Buffalo. Those police have not rendered aid to the man whose life they themselves jeopardized."

"No profession wants to have bad apples."

This legislation is transformative."

"Part of the movement about defunding is about how we use resources. How we define public safety."

"Our moral standards have been demonized, jeopardized. The demonstrations are thus justified."

GET YOUR KNEE
OFF OUR NECKS

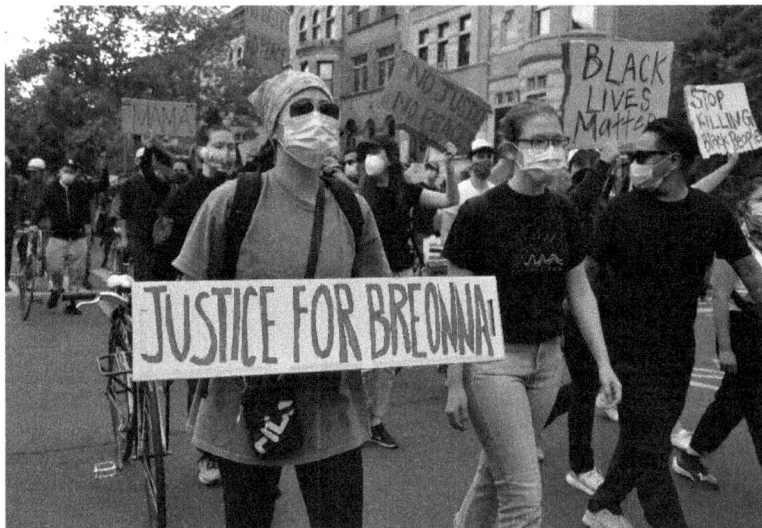

Get your Knee off Our Necks – Photo –

JEH JOHNSON – Former Chairman Department of Homeland Security – "What can poor leadership accomplish, Nothing."

"We must embrace the grievances that is being demonstrated."

"There is need for national leadership that needs to acknowledge the grievances being expressed."

"In 2008, we all believed this was a defining moment. Much of that optimism was dampened. This administration wants to take us several steps backward."

FREDERICK MONDERSON

Get your Knee off Our Necks – Photo –

"Its not a matter of training but the kind of people we are recruiting. We must recruit people who want to protect and serve."

"The neighborhood bully is not a good example of what a policeman should be."

GET YOUR KNEE
OFF OUR NECKS

"One incident has the ability to undermine your whole operation in a community."

"'Bitterness grows into hopelessness' as my grandfather Charles S. Johnson used to say."

Minneapolis is not a black problem. It is an American problem. We must recognize, the protest has gone global!"

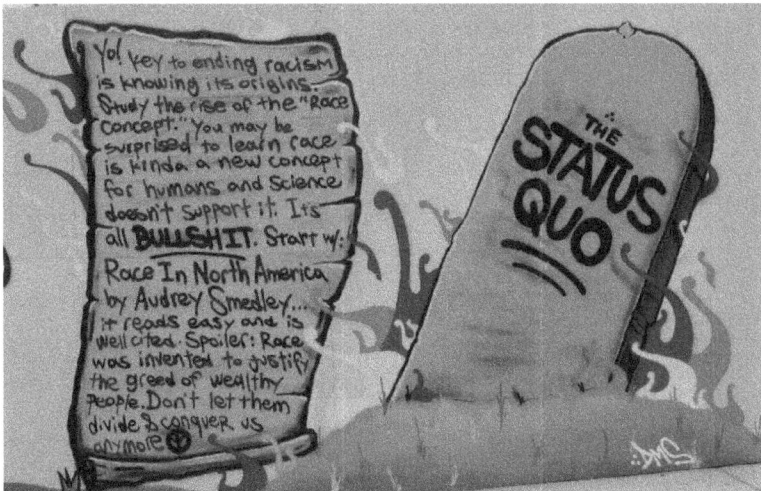

Get your Knee off Our Necks – Photo –

FAREED ZAKARIA – "Donald Trump started by saying his Inauguration crowd was the largest ever. Spicer repeated it. He's been called the greatest President. He relishes in the best unemployment figures, though he does not take responsibility for the 40 million unemployed. He said China would pay for the Tariffs and even that Windmills cause cancer. Republicans repeat

Trump's lies. They are thus considered, cheerful collaborators."

CHARLES BLOW – We need to recognize "The power and danger of despair."

"Despair is a dangerous condition."

"We could believe, people could conceive this amount of despair and desperation."

"There is no mention of the Police in the Constitution. We created the police. The Supreme Court set up the idea of police action as reasonable fear."

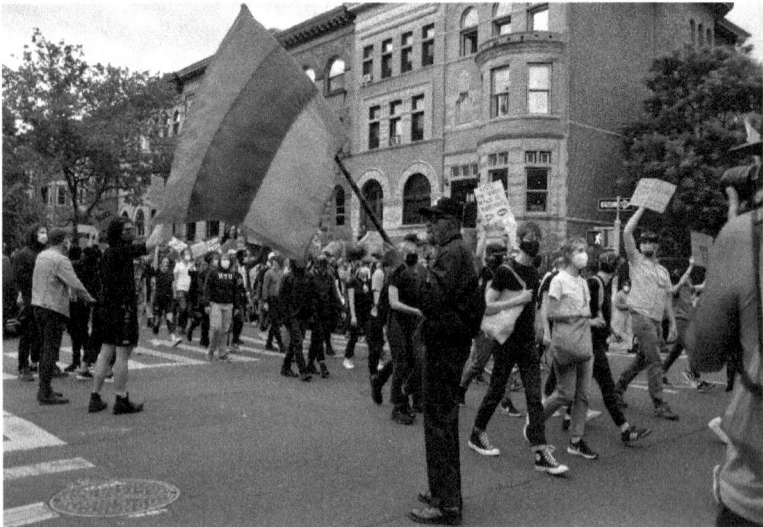

Get your Knee off Our Necks – Photo –

GET YOUR KNEE
OFF OUR NECKS

"Floyd is the last, the straw that broke the camel's back."

"Tamika Mallory, the civil rights activist, represented despair and desperation. Amaud Arbery – no arrest for two months. Kendricks – waited two months. Only when people spoke up did we get a credible response. Floyd calling his dead mother. America has caused a level of trauma Dr. King, Ida B. Wells, Rosa Parks and Jesse Jackson, all tried to warn us about. Beneath it all is systemic racism."

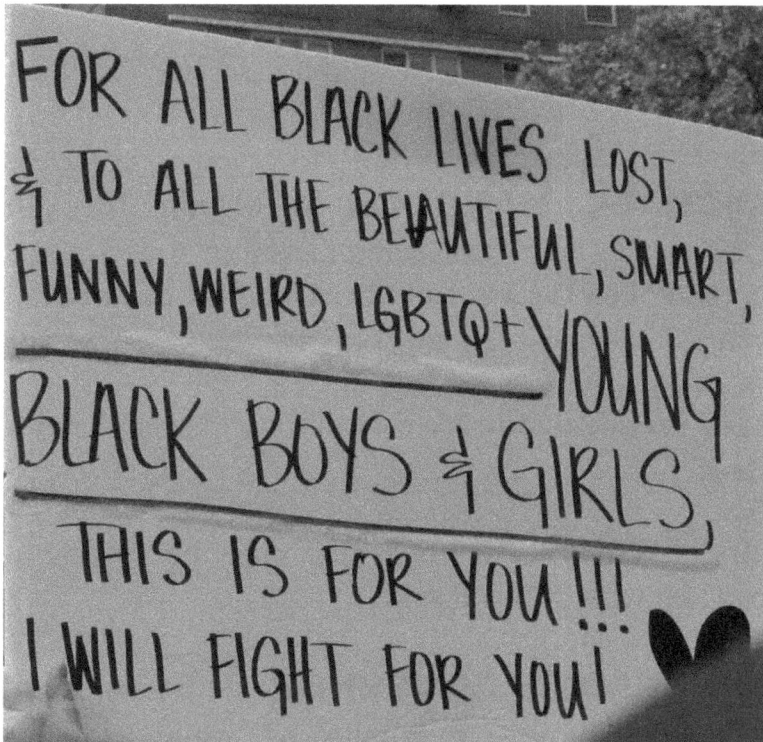

Get your Knee off Our Necks – Photo –

FREDERICK MONDERSON

GWEN CARR – "I spoke to the Floyd family. I have a broken heart. When I saw this, it was like my son screaming from the Grave."

POLICE CHIEF JORGE COLINO – Miami Police Department. "This is the first time in my 30 years I have seen so many unions and Police Chiefs come out and call this for what it is, murder."

"It is easy to charge an officer but to convict is another thing."

"The police must have public service in their hearts."

MICHAEL HANCOCK – Mayor, City of Denver – "There is systemic racism in America and in the Police Department. Its existed for hundreds of years."

"The president must have credibility to speak on this issue."

"It can't just be words. There must be actions to back up what is being said."

MINNESOTA GOVERNOR – "Blacks don't have the same opportunity as whites in this country."

GET YOUR KNEE
OFF OUR NECKS

DR. LEONARD JAMES – "Here we're seeing the scab of the sore being peeled back and all the ugly pus of racism, discrimination and denial oozing to stain the image of America in the eyes of the world."

BAKARI SELLERS – "I want my daughter to know, my father's path and mine are woven over this bloody ground."

"One of the greatest flaws in this country is the absence of empathy!"

"What are you teaching, Empathy, Compassion?"

Get your Knee off Our Necks – Photo –

FREDERICK MONDERSON

WES MOORE – "What examples are white parents setting for their children who are watching them?"

"I want you to use the same aggression you use to protect your child as you would for my child."

"Twelve times the National Guards were called out. Ten times were for race."

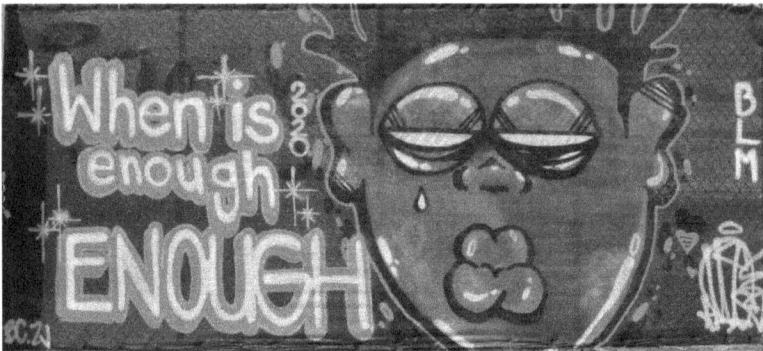

Get your Knee off Our Necks – Photo –

MICHAEL HANCOCK – "I want to be treated as a human being.'

"We have to vote."

"We have to restructure the system."

GET YOUR KNEE
OFF OUR NECKS

"I want to work, love, to live in peace. We must have a Police Department that is empathetic to assume the worse."

"We have to go to Congress. We have to be strategic."

SABRINA FULTON - "When there is loss of life there needs to be a complete examination of an arrest."

"We no longer feel safe in our own community, in our own country."

"When a toxicology test is done on the victim, the same test must be done on the person who shot him."

MICHAEL JORDAN – "Pledges $100,000,000.00 (One hundred Million Dollars) over the next ten years to promote racial equality."

FREDERICK MONDERSON

Get your Knee off Our Necks – Photo –

SENATOR CORY BOOKER – "Change doesn't come from Washington; Change comes to Washington."

JOHN HARWOOD – "The president projects an image of a tough guy."

REPRESENTATIVE SHEILA JACKSON - "We want our country back."

"We hear you."

REV. REMUS WRIGHT – "Grieving in light of such a tragedy, it is hard for you go "from astonishment, grief, anger, outrage." Then you must deal with the reality of what happened.

GET YOUR KNEE
OFF OUR NECKS

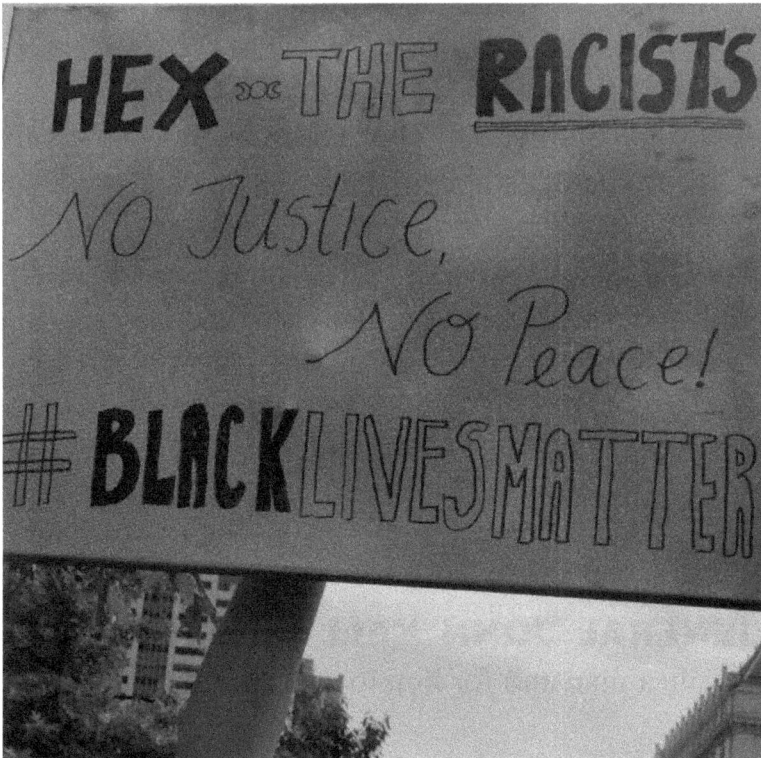

Get your Knee off Our Necks – Photo –

GOVERNOR ABBOTT – (R) TEXAS – "It is the most horrific tragedy I have ever observed. I will make sure this does not happen in Texas." Yes, but it did happen in Texas, Governor. I happened in 2019 and a video is now coming to light.

"We must make sure George Floyd did not die in vain. George Floyd's death will fundamentally change America."

FREDERICK MONDERSON

SHERIFF HUBERT PETERKIN – "We are part of the problem." "We have to know we are part of the problem."

DAVID GREGORY – "The photo-op so loudly criticized was one of the low points of his Presidency."

KWAME TURE – "If you want to lynch me, that's your problem. If you have the power to lynch me, that's my problem."

GENERAL JOHN KELLY – "General Mattis is quite a man and for him to do that it tells a lot."

GENERAL COLIN POWELL - "**He lies**. He is not an effective president. This is dangerous for the country. He has drifted away from the Constitution."

"It is indeed strange that General Mike Mullen, Admiral Dempsey, General Allen, General Mattis and General Kelly, all express dismay and repugnance at what President Donald Trump has done to this nation, its Constitution and the American people."

GET YOUR KNEE
OFF OUR NECKS

Get your Knee off Our Necks – Photo –

OMAR JIMMINEZ – "Mr. Floyd's death is the beginning of a Legacy."

JAMES CLYBURN – "Sure we took a knee, but for 244 years the oppressor has been on the necks of Blacks who came to this country."

FANNIE LOU HAMER – "I'm sick and tired of being sick and tired."

VERNA MYERS – "Whites think they're superior to others because of the society."

"Implicit bias and racism are interconnected."

"The police are 5-times more likely to kill a black man than a white man."

"Bias is not about looking at one incident or issue but at a number of factors."

VAN JONES – "Threatening no one; but threatened, yet still seen as a threat."

ANNA NAVARO – "Ignorance and racism has a huge correlation."

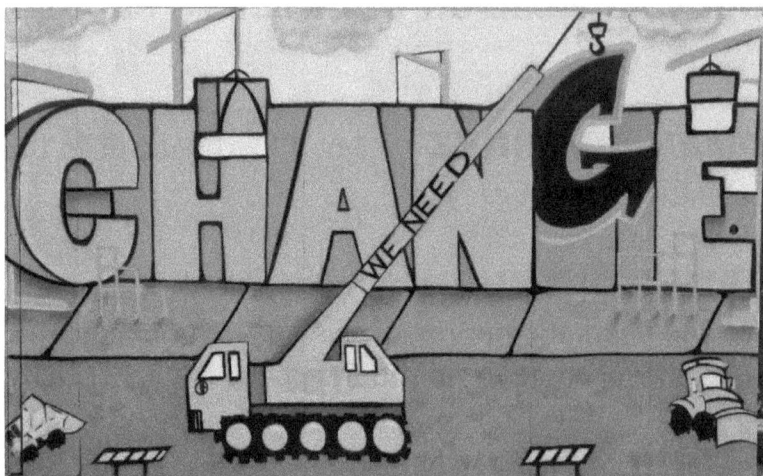

Get your Knee off Our Necks – Photo –

"I see things now I didn't see before."

ROBIN DiANGELO – "The message is clear in this society that from as early as 3 or 4, 'Its better to be white.'"

GET YOUR KNEE
OFF OUR NECKS

"The implicit bias of a Black man is not as significant on a white man/woman who has the whole system at their back."

ANONYMOUS – "What if I say the wrong thing!"

HAKEEM JEFFRIES – "Joe Biden cares more for the African-American community than is coming out of the White House."

JOE BIDEN – "I won't be trafficking in fear and division."

ABBY PHILIPS – "Biden's message is about governance. How you run the government and the president has failed thus far."

FREDERICK MONDERSON

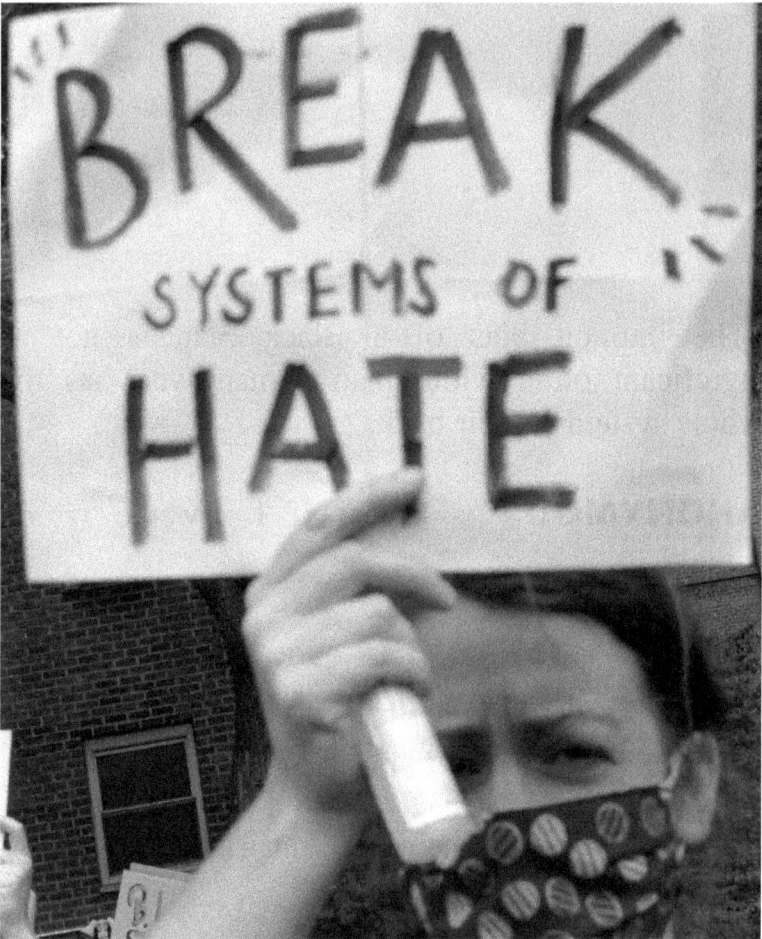

Get your Knee off Our Necks – Photo –

JAMES CLYBURN - "A black running mate is a "plus" not a "must" for Biden.

SAMUEL A. JACKSON – "We're not saying Black Lives are more important. We're only saying **BLACK LIVES MATTER!**"

GET YOUR KNEE
OFF OUR NECKS

"It is amazing. I'm energized watching them do it."

"In my mind I feel we're about to see change."

"I do believe change can happen but it won't be immediate. It will take time."

"The water broke. We're in labor now. Let's see what you can do!"

"Patience is voting in the right mayor, who hires the right chief who hires the right captain to do the right job."

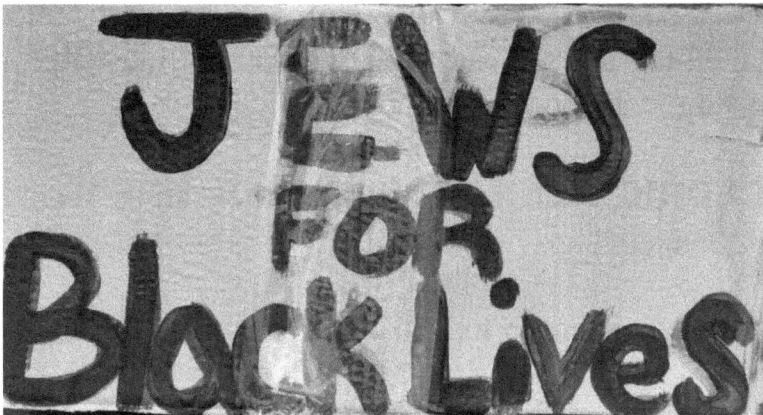

Get your Knee off Our Necks – Photo –

DONALD TRUMP – "I went down to inspect the bunker. I only spent a little, small, tiny time there."

FREDERICK MONDERSON

ATTORNEY GENERAL WILLIAM BARR
– "Things had gotten so bad; the Secret Service took the President to the Bunker."

COLIN POWELL – "HE LIES!"

BAKARI SELLERS – Asinine, ignorant, intellectual dishonesty. He chastises "Take a knee," but supports Confederate Generals" who dishonored the flag, threatened the Constitution, disrupted the union, even killed Americans."

"He just spews a bunch of nothing rather than inject himself into any meaningful discussion."

GLORIA BORGER – "Mr. trump is unable, unwilling and refuses to engage in any meaningful dialogue. He lives in a bubble."

CEDRIC ALEXANDER – "Chokeholds should be banned."

"Chokeholds need to be banned, period."

"If there's an extenuating circumstance, then that officer needs to explain it."

DAVID MACATEE - Don't poke the bear. We need a national, a world, leader."

GET YOUR KNEE
OFF OUR NECKS

REPUBLIC VOTER – "Biden is a decent, kind man."

DR. JONATHAN REINER – "This is an irreconcilable conflict of interest because the president is running for reelection.

"Can't sue! If you can't get COVID, then 'Drop the Disclaimer' He's holding a rally in a hot zone."

MARTIN LUTHER KING, JR. – "We will not remember the words of our enemies but the silence of our friends."

ANONYMOUS - PROTESTERS SHUT DOWN PART OF I-395

SPIKE LEE – "Deeds not words."

"This is for real."

"We have to register and come out and vote."

"Move forward together."

FREDERICK MONDERSON

Get your Knee off Our Necks – Photo –

REV. AL SHARPTON – "When he took his last breath, we began to breathe."

JOE BIDEN – "Now is the time for racial justice."

CORNELL WEST – "We will breathe."

"There was no reference to hate or revenge."

"After George Floyd, Martin Luther King, Fannie Lou Hamer, we have to wonder."

"We're losing but we have to continue fighting."

"These are crimes, police crimes."

GET YOUR KNEE
OFF OUR NECKS

"Hope in the form of love, but get ready for Neofascist backlash."

"Can we hold on to integrity, honesty and decency."

MALCOLM X – "Sincerity is my only credentials."

Get your Knee off Our Necks – Photo –

CONGRESSMAN HAKEEM JEFFRIES – "Chokeholds are uncivilized, unconscionable. It is an un-American form of policing."

"It is unlawful as a matter of policy. We need to make it a matter of law."

FREDERICK MONDERSON

KENDRICK PERKINS – "It is murder by police. We can change the system. We need a master plan, a power plan to achieve this."

PROF. GLORIA BROWN MARSHALL – "He could not have invoked a worse symbol in Frank Rizzo."

LEBRON JAMES – MORE THAN A VOTE - PROTECT THE VOTE – "We must register and vote."

"We must fight voter suppression."

ANONYMOUS – "NASCAR, NFL and Corporate America must act on police brutality and killings."

MAYA ANGELOU – "When you know better, do better."

JOE BIDEN – "The country is crying out for leadership; leadership that brings us together."

KEISHA LANCE-BOTTOMS – MAYOR OF ATLANTA – "We must articulate more than our anger. We want more for our children and their children."

GET YOUR KNEE
OFF OUR NECKS

Get your Knee off Our Necks – Photo –

GENERAL JOHN KELLY – "I think we need to think harder of the people who we elect."

MAGGIE HABERMAN – "If people of substance speak out, then the President will be forced to act correctly."

"While Mr. Trump may be able to build a fortress around the White House, he won't be able to build a fortress around his presidency."

FREDERICK MONDERSON

"Former presidents speak out in contrast to Trump's approach."

DONALD TRUMP – "I am your president of law and order!"

ANONYMOUS - "Trump stokes disunity as protests grip the nation."

ABBY PHILIPS - "His attempts to clear the streets galvanized the people. There were lots of people who were anti-Trump, anti-racism, anti-police. That is the crowd he is now trying to downplay."

DWIGHT HOWARD – "I don't want anything to distract us!"

Get your Knee off Our Necks – Photo –

GET YOUR KNEE
OFF OUR NECKS

URSULA BURNS – "You are the architects of a system in crisis that you benefit from with privileges. Today that system needs fixing, yet you're asking me how to fix it."

"You must change this system. You must talk to your people and try to fix it."

"Police yourself!"

"How long can we wait?"

"US Companies must dismantle racial imbalances."

MARY BROOKS – "We're being killed by people we pay!"

DUSTIN ROBERTS – "Swift appropriate action is needed."

JAMES CLYBURN - "Nobody is going to defund the police. We can restructure the police."

MARY BROOKS – "Clyburn may fear the police but we cannot allow the next generation to inherit that fear."

"The system is rotten to the core. Retraining won't do much."

CEDRIC ALEXANDER – "There is denial around the question of racism. It exists in every institution in this country."

KEISHA LANCE-BOTTOMS - There are two diseases operating now – Racism and Coronavirus."

STEPHANIE RAWLINS BLAKE – "Donald Trump will never ever consider changes to his beliefs. He is missing a huge opportunity to lead, heal and truly be the President of all the people."

"Something has touched the conscience of the nation of human species."

"When **NASCAR** has changed its behavior, this is significant."

GET YOUR KNEE
OFF OUR NECKS

Get your Knee off Our Necks – Photo –

J.C. WATTS – "Amaud Arbery was the Tipping Point and George Floyd the Turning Point."

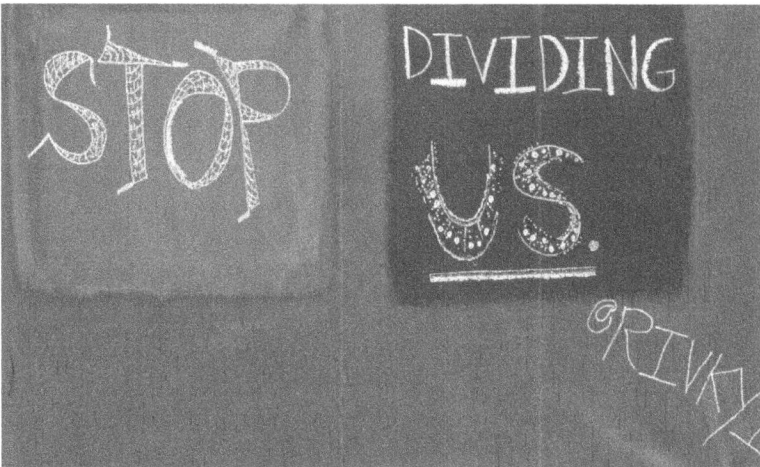

Get your Knee off Our Necks – Photo –

DOUGLAS BRINKLEY – "Why does Mr. Trump hire such losers."

DOUGLAS BRINKLEY ON BOLTON - "Why would you hire a washed-up person to run American foreign policy."

"Mr. Trump is an incompetent president with a deep authoritarian bent."

"Donald Trump is an autocrat."

JEFFREY TOOBIN – "Shocking but not surprising."

"The Supreme Court stood up to Trump's authoritarian behavior."

DOUGLAS BRINKLEY – "Donald Trump is a sickening conspiracy monger. The question is, 'Can our institutions survive Trump.' He is not right in the head."

"The stakes are higher in 2020. People are getting set to vote at higher numbers in 2020."

ASTEAD HERNDON – "There isn't a path for moderates on the national stage without the input of people of color."

GET YOUR KNEE
OFF OUR NECKS

JEREMY DIAMOND - "There are multiple crises happening at the same time. People are in the streets, the Carona-virus Pandemic is expanding, two Supreme Court ruling were made against Donald Trump and now Bolton has stated Trump is 'Not fit for office.'"

DONALD TRUMP - "I made Juneteenth famous."

ANONYMOUS – "We have heard 'follow the leader, follow the leader. Now were hearing 'follow the liar, follow the liar."

Get your Knee off Our Necks – Photo –

HOUSTON MAYOR – "Demonstrators have caused immediate action."

BEN JEALOUS – "Donald Trump must rise in this moment as President."

"We must fight for equality and fight against hatred and slavery."

MAX BOOT – "Donald Trump is assaulting the rule of law every day."

JOHN HARWOOD – "With Mattis, Kelly and Powell, with what we see, it's not in serious doubt, Donald Trump is not up to the job."

JAMES CLYBURN – "Don't let **Defund the Police** highjack momentum for **Reform**. **Restructure don't Defund**."

JEH JOHNSON – "Its not a matter of training, but the people we're recruiting."

GET YOUR KNEE OFF OUR NECKS

Get your Knee off Our Necks – Photo –

BEN FRANKLIN – "A Republic, if you can keep it."

CARL BERNSTEIN – "Trump's race baiting, religious bigotry and destruction of the truth is an expression of power."

CHARLES S. JOHNSON – "Bitterness grows out of hopelessness."

GENERAL ALLEN – "That is what happens in authoritarian countries."

KAYLEIGH MCENANY – "There is no regrets on part of this White House."

FREDERICK MONDERSON

BUBBA WATSON – You're not going to take away my smile!"

GENERAL HAYDEN – "I said this was not happening in America."

"The first time in my life, I'm worried about my country."

DAN RATHER – "There have been lots of crises in our nation's history, but never in our history has our leader been absent without leave."

JOHN HARWOOD – "Leadership has just cut and run."

MITCH LANDRIEU – "I was born at night but not last night."

"Blacks see George Floyd's killing as America's knee on their necks."

"He played the Race Card as a Dog-whistle."

STERLING HIGGINS – "These issues have moved past the president. Shame on him."

"There is systemic racism."

GET YOUR KNEE
OFF OUR NECKS

STEVIE WONDER – "All lives matter, but only when **Black Lives Matter**."

Get your Knee off Our Necks – Photo –

10. ROLL CALL OF BLACKS MURDERED BY POLICE

ALTON STERLIN

SAMUEL DUBOSE

TERENCE CUTCHEN

FREDERICK MONDERSON

KEILLART SCOTT

STEPHON CLARK

BOTHEN JEAN

ALATIANA JEFFREY

ERIK HARRISON

AMAUD ARBERY

WALTER SCOTT

DAVID MACATE

FREDDIE GRAY

SANDRA BLAND

ERIC GARNER

AMADOU DIALLO

SEAN BELL

GET YOUR KNEE
OFF OUR NECKS

TANIC SCOTT

JOHN CRAWFORD III

Get your Knee off Our Necks – Photo –

ARTHUR MILLER

RAYSHARD BROOKS

ERIK LOGAN

MICHAEL BROWN

PAMELA TURNER

FREDERICK MONDERSON

BREONNA TAYLOR

WALTER SCOTT

TAMIR RICE

ALI GRAVES

DAVID MACATEE

TONY MCDADE

JOE ACEVDEO

CARLOS INGRAM LOPEZ

EZELL FORD

DANTE PARKER

MICHELLE CUSSEAUX

LAQUAN MCDONALD

GEORGE MANN

GET YOUR KNEE
OFF OUR NECKS

TANISHA ANDERSON

AKAI GURLEY

RUMAIN BRUSBON

JERAME REID

MATTHEW AJIBADE

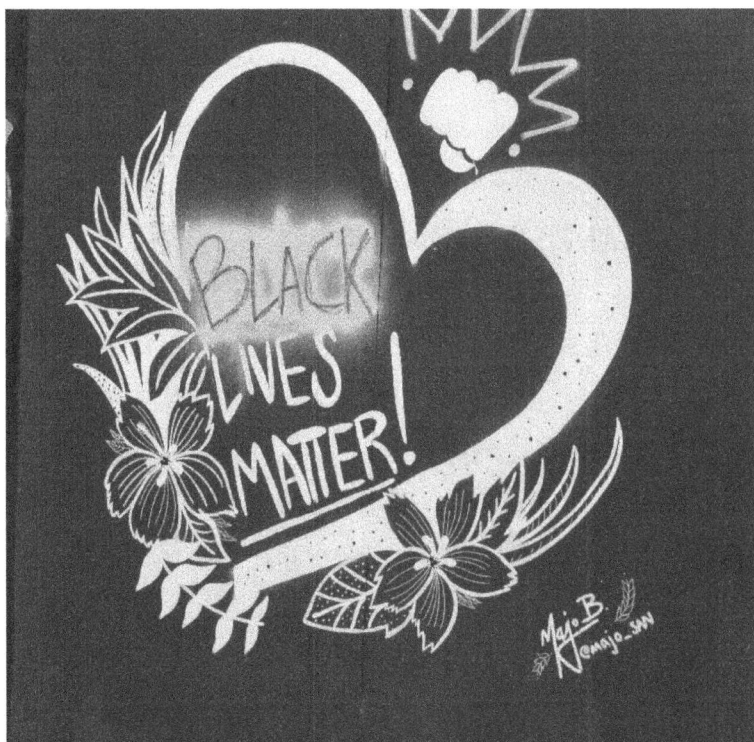

Get your Knee off Our Necks – Photo –

FREDERICK MONDERSON

FRANK SMART

NATASHA MCKENNA

TONY ROBINSON

ANTHONY HILL

MAYA HALL

PHILIP WHITE

ERIC HARRIS

WILLIAM CHAPMAN III

ALEXA CHRISTIAN

BRENDON GLENN

VICTOR MANUEL LAROSA

JONATHAN SANDERS

FREDDIE BULE

GET YOUR KNEE
OFF OUR NECKS

JOSEPH MANN

Get your Knee off Our Necks – Photo –

DARIUS STEWART

BILLY RAY DAVIS

MICHAEL SABBLE

BRIAN KEITH DAY

CHRISTIAN TAYLOR

TROY ROBINSON

FREDERICK MONDERSON

INDIA KAZER

ASHAMS PHARAOH MANLEY

GRLIX KUMI

KEITH HARRISON MCNEDD

JUNOYL PROSPER

LAMONTEX JONES

AYANA JONES

PHILANDO CASTILE

CHRISTOPHER WHITEFIELD

PAUL ORTEGA

RICHARD PERKINS

GET YOUR KNEE
OFF OUR NECKS

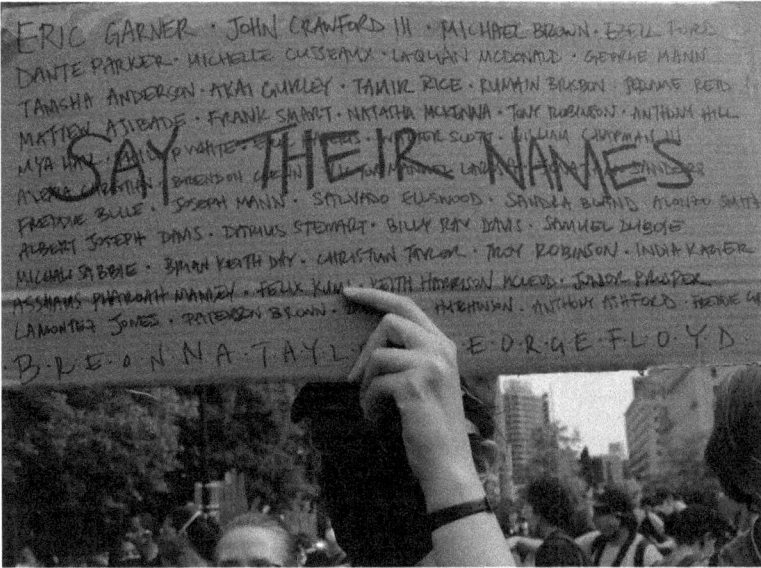

Get your Knee off Our Necks – Photo –

BETTIE JONES

MIGUEL ESPINAL

CHRISTOPHER MCCORNEY

BRENDO GLENN

GEORGE MANN

BILLY RAY DAVIS

FREDERICK MONDERSON

ANTHONY ASKFORD

PETERSON BROWN

LAVANNIE BIGGS

STEPHON CLARKE

Get your Knee off Our Necks – Photo –

SYVLLIS SMITHS

MATHEW AJIBADE

RANDON NELSON

GET YOUR KNEE
OFF OUR NECKS

JONATHAN SANDERS

ALTERIA WOODS

RANDY NELSON

WALTER SCOTT

TEMPHILL THOMAS

INNA HAGER

ALONZO SMITH

NATASHA MCKENNA

MICHAEL LEE MARSHALL

WENDELL CELESTINE

LA'VON BIGGS

MARIO TRUXIBO

PETER GAINES

FREDERICK MONDERSON

VALBERT JOSEPH DAVIS

BOTHAW JEAN

RUMAN BRISHON

RONELL FOSTER

COLIN ROQUEMORE QUINTORIO

CHRISTOPHER DAVIS

BLACK LIVES REALLY DO FUCKING MATTER

GET YOUR KNEE OFF OUR NECKS

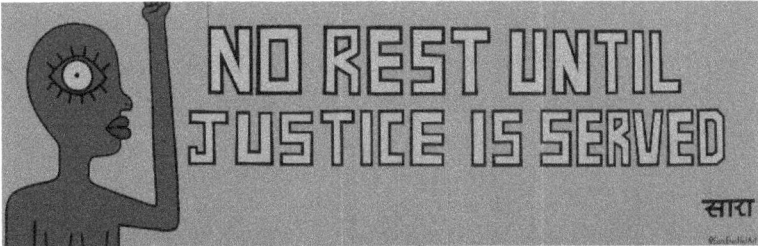

Get your Knee off Our Necks – Photo –

11. "SHUT YOUR MOUTH!" BY DR. FRED MONDERSON

After former President Barack Obama issued a scathing condemnation of the Trump Administration's response to the Coronavirus COVID-19 Pandemic describing it as an "absolute disaster," Senate Majority Leader Mitch McConnell responded, "The President should shut his mouth!" Naturally, "Moscow Mitch" knows a lot about open and shut mouths.

President Obama spoke out against President Trump in light of 80,000 American deaths from the Coronavirus because the present administration bungled its response to the virus. Mr. Obama's stance was necessary given Republican leadership has remained silent in response to Donald trump's poor leadership. More important, however, in Mr. Obama's case the Office of the Presidency he worked unending for 8-years to protect and improve its moral stature, dignity and leadership efficacy has declined precipitously because Trump messed things up, particularly with his cesspool of lies and other obnoxious actions.

Get your Knee off Our Necks – Photo –

No less significant, Mitch McConnell has not been shy at opening his mouth, but to say the wrong things as in this and so many cases. For example, in 2008 right after the nation elected the first African-American President, Barack Obama, Mr. McConnell was quick to open his mouth to say, "I intend to make Barack Obama a one term president!" Notice how he took on the full weight of this responsibility as one with a gigantic ego. Naturally he failed, but

GET YOUR KNEE
OFF OUR NECKS

proverbially he failed and with his cohorts not only did they, as one writer called it, "Lynched Obama," block his every legislative initiative designed to rescue the nation from the depths of despair the previous Republican administration created, but encouraged racist and disrespectful attitudes and behaviors towards a decent human being blest with elegance of mind and nobility of spirit. Morgan Freeman, the academy award winning actor, on Piers Morgan TV Show, called McConnell's words "blatantly racist."

That McConnell's mouth remained open through the 2012 reelection success of Mr. Obama attests to his failure to deliver on the plot of treason. In October 2013, in a "big write-up" *The New York Times* newspaper detailed the ongoing plot against Mr. Obama by Republicans and Mr. McConnell was a leading figure. In fact, Chris Cillizza chronicled Mr. McConnell's fifty-year rise with aspirations to become Senate Majority leader in which he called him a "Plotter." Hence, it's easy to see his role in "plots against Obama." Without question, and even later, photographs of "Republican Who's Who" involved were exposed on CNN for their role in attempts to overthrow the legitimate and respected Obama Presidency.

Such persons as "Waterloo" Jim DeMint; "You lie" Joe Wilson; "Stupid" Chuck Grassley among others, in concert with the "Tea Party" movement and the "Party of No" Cabal blocked every legislative initiative of the Obama administration as it grappled with the nation's economic woes magnified in the 2008 Recession. Mr. McConnell did keep his mouth shut as this great President wilted under Republican-American "friendly fire."

Get your Knee off Our Necks – Photo –

In a disgusting gaffe, Mr. McConnell opened his mouth to boast on the Public Airwaves, "I looked Obama in the eye and said, 'Mr. President. You will not get this judgeship,' to fill Mr. Kennedy's seat despite the fact Justice Garland was highly qualified for the position. Further demonstrating he oral diarrhea, "Moscow Mitch" exposed his hand in glove association with Donald Trump emphasizing their selection, nomination and appointment of "conservative judges," unmindful such appointments compromised these individuals' judicial objectivity and integrity. One of his talking

GET YOUR KNEE
OFF OUR NECKS

points during Mr. Garland consideration was, "This is an election year" and so let the voters decide. Yet, when it came to fill Justice Scalia's seat with Judge Kavanaugh, Mitch was the point man. Even more sad, opening his mouth again on the airwaves, when asked if another judgeship became vacant before the end of President Trump's term, what would he do; "Mouth Open, Story Jump Out Mitch" said, "I would fill it immediately." This particularly statement betrays two failures or shortfalls of Senator Mitch McConnell. Not only has he publicly demonstrated usurping the president's responsibility to fill a judgeship, but his failure to become president, despite his "50 years in politics" as a plotter is probably why he behaved so uncivil towards Barack Obama.

Mr. Obama "opened his mouth" because he believed America is suffering in unrelenting assault from the White House during which Mr. McConnell and Republican associates stay silent to the ongoing travesty. More important, when Mitch stands with colleagues before the "Mike" in the halls of government and make their insidious remarks couched in code words what we see is stern-faced white men in positions of power who represent the racist core of the American racist timber. While we are not familiar with some of Mr. McConnell's "open mouth" pronouncements as he rests comfortably in bed with Donald Trump who equally spouts "fine people on both sides," he remains "closed mouth" about Mr. Trump's more than

20,000 lies and false statements; his perennial behavior as "equal opportunity insulter;" failed leadership in the 130,000 deaths from the Coronavirus calamity; his propensity as an "under the bus thrower" given his perennially "I don't know that person" mantra; his reckless calls to open the economy at all costs because his businesses are not doing so well; his blatant disregard of the scientific community's insistence on caution in all actions; Mr. Trump's refusal to release his tax returns which would expose his financial connections to foreign entities as an indication of how he and his family are benefitting from exploiting the presidency for personal gain or whether he is indebted to foreign entities that impact on his presidential obligations; his abuse of the White House Coronavirus daily Taskforce Briefings to campaign for reelection given his dismal leadership or lack thereof poses a problem for his re-election.

Mr. Obama spoke up because the American house is on fire and Senate Majority Mitch McConnell and colleagues, failed in their responsibility to the nation, have not only remained silent, they're as Abraham Lincoln has prophetically acclaimed, "Silence in face of an injustice is complicity in that injustice." Fortunately, however, history will not remain silent but will open its mouth to castigate miscreants of the age of Donald Trump who, given the opportunity to lead this great nation and write upon the pages of history spilled the ink, blotted the

GET YOUR KNEE
OFF OUR NECKS

pages and indelibly stamped the record with racist and substandard leadership while pandering to the likes of white supremacist, KKK, far right and other such savory characters, led by the "Equal Opportunity Abuser" himself, Donald John Trump.

Get your Knee off Our Necks – Photo –

12.   SIGNS

BLACK LIVES MATTER

I CAN'T BREATHE

JUSTICE FOR GEORGE FLOYD

JUSTICE FOR BREONNA

STOP KILLING BLACK MEN

LATINAS FOR BLACK LIVES MATTER

BLM

WE STILL CAN'T BREATHE

WHITE SILENCE IS VIOLENCE

STOP KILLING US

I HEAR YOU - I SEE YOU

MY LIFE MATTERS

GET YOUR KNEE
OFF OUR NECKS

STOP KILLING BLACK PEOPLE

SKIN COLOR SHOULDN'T BE A DEATH
SENTENCE

FORWARD EVER, BACKWARD NEVER

GET YOUR KNEE OFF OUR NECKS

WE ARE DONE DYING

NO JUSTICE, NO PEACE

KNOW JUSTICE, KNOW PEACE

STOP VOTING FOR ELITEIST RACISTS

ENOUGH IS ENOUGH

FREDERICK MONDERSON

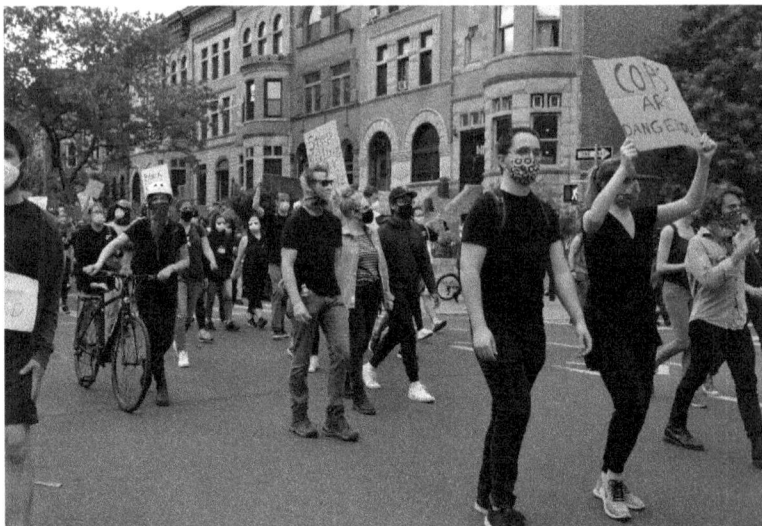

Get your Knee off Our Necks – Photo –

CALL FOR RACIAL JUSTICE SPREADING AROUND THE WORLD

WE ARE FACING THREE PANDEMICS – HEALTH, ECONOMIC, RACIAL

THE MAKE UP OF PROTESTERS DEMONSTRATES THEY ARE SERIOUSLY FED UP WITH THE INJUSTICE AND DONT WANT TO LIVE UNDER THESE SYSTEMS

BE MY VOCE

RACISM IS PANDEMIC

GET YOUR KNEE
OFF OUR NECKS

TRUMP EQUALS PLAGUE

NEED FOR JUSTICE

THE TIDE HAS TURNED

WE'RE ALL GEORGE

STOP KARENS FROM BREEDING

SOCIAL DISTANCING

NO JUSTICE, NO PEACE

I AM A MAN!

A MAN WAS LYNCHED YESTERDAY

POLICE KILLING UNARMED BLACK PEOPLE

NO LESSONS LEARNED

BLACK TRANS-LIVES MATTER

FREDERICK MONDERSON

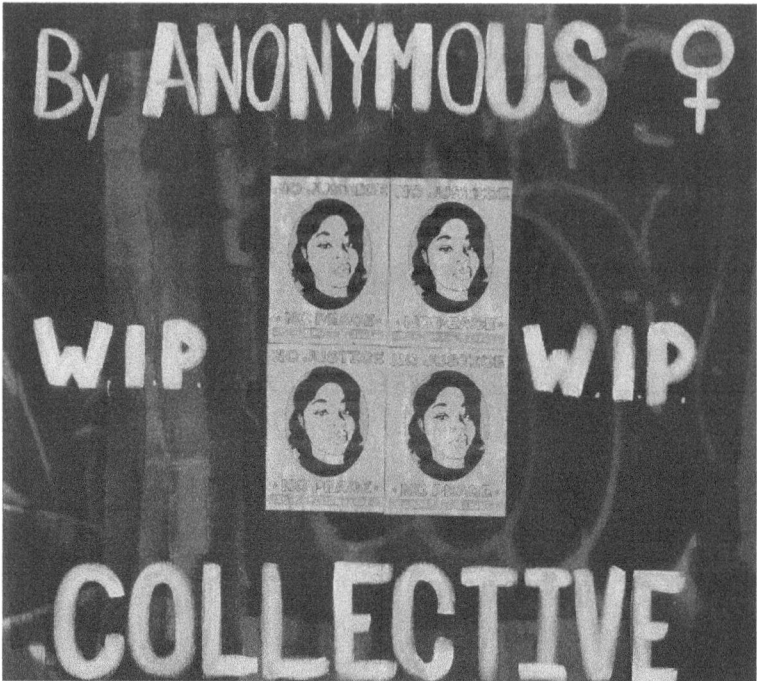

Get your Knee off Our Necks – Photo –

TALK TO YOUR RACIST AUNT

STOP THE PAIN

LISTEN TO THE CALL

STOP US BEING TIRED

JUSTICE NOW

GET YOUR KNEE
OFF OUR NECKS

NOW MORE THAT EVER BLACK LIVES
MATTER

TRUMP FATIGUE

COLOR ME TRUE

LET US BREATHE

BLESS YOUR HEART

TOGETHER

REACTION

PROUDLY SERVING IN THE WAR ON
INJUSTICE

WE ARE TIRED OF THIS

FREDERICK MONDERSON

Get your Knee off Our Necks – Photo –

JUNETEENTH BLACK LIVES MATTER

WHITE LIVES MATTER – SO TOO DO BLACK LIVES MATTER

BLACK LIVES ARE BEING KILLED, NOT WHITE LIVES ARE BEING KILLED

JUSTICE FOR BROOKS

BLACK LIVES MATTER TOO

GET YOUR KNEE
OFF OUR NECKS

IN UNITY FOR CHANGE

JUSTICE FOR ANDROS

STOP KILLING OUR BROTHERS AND SISTERS

BLACK SOLIDARITY

Get your Knee off Our Necks – Photo –

STOP KILLING US

WE'RE GOING TO FIGHT FOR SOCIAL JUSTICE

FREDERICK MONDERSON

ASIANS FOR BLM

CELEBRATE BLACK JOY, TEACH AND SUPPORT BLACK HISTORY

WHAT WILL IT TAKE

MORE CARE, LESS COPS

WE LOVE OUR BLACK TRANS

BACK GENOCIDE 1619-2020

TOO BUSY TO HATE

RENEWAL AND REFORM

END RACISM NOW

FIGHT THE POWER

CORRUPT

BILL BARR LIED TO THE AMERICAN PEOPLE

GET YOUR KNEE
OFF OUR NECKS

JUSTICE

HISTORY HAS ITS EYES ON YOU

COPS MURDERED GEORGE FLOYD

NOT POLICE BRUTALITY BUT KILLING

LOVE GEORGE

Get your Knee off Our Necks – Photo –

PREVENT MASS GATHERING, STOP KILLING BLACK PEOPLE

FREDERICK MONDERSON

JUSTICE 4 FLOYD

DEATH SENTENCE # 1087

LIFE 4 # 7162

SHUT IT DOWN

POLICE > CITIZENS

HIS NAME IS GEORGE FLOYD

STOP KILLING BLACK PEOPLE

END WHITE SUPREMACY

MPD = MURDERERS

"PLEASE, I CAN'T BREATHE. THE KNEE ON MY NECK, I CAN'T BREATE, OFFICER. THEY GONNA KILL ME." GEORGE FLOYD

MAMA

GET YOUR KNEE
OFF OUR NECKS

FTP

HIS NAME WAS GEORGE FLOYD

ABOLISH THE POLICE

MPLS POLICE KILLS ANOTHER BLACK MAN – "I CAN'T BREATHE"

THOU SHALL NOT KILL

POWER TO PEOPLE

THE JUSTICE SYSTEM IS CRIMINAL

I CAN'T BREATHE – BLACK LIVES MATTER

I CAN'T BREATHE – JUSTICE FOR FLOYD

FIST UP, AFRO OUT

RACISM IS PANDEMIC

RACISM IS A PANDEMIC TOO. RIP GF

FREDERICK MONDERSON

SILENCE IS NOT AN OPTION

HEX THE RACISTS NO JUSTICE NO PEACE # BLACK LIVES MATTER

BLACK LIVES MATTER # BLM @LOVE.EVERY.SOUL

FOR ALL BLACK LIVES LOST AND TO ALL THE BEAUTIFUL, SMART, FUNNY, WEIRD, LGBTQ AND YOUNG – BLACK BOYS AND GIRLS – THIS IS FOR YOU!!! - I WILL FIGHT FOR YOU!

GET YOUR KNEE OFF OUR NECKS

Get your Knee off our Necks – Photo –

"INJUSTICE ANYWHERE IS A THREAT TO JUSTICE EVERYWHERE"

SAY HIS NAME

GEORGE FLOYD

FREDERICK MONDERSON

DEFUND THE POLICE

"BRAKE" SYSTEMS OF HATE

"BUILD" LOVE WITH EQUALITY

41 SHOTS

Get your Knee off Our Necks – Photo –

WITH LIBERTY AND JUSTICE FOR ALL – RIP GEORGE FLOYD (LOVE) # BLM

FROM MINNEAPOLIS TO JERUSALEM END SYSTEMIC RACISM - BLACK

GET YOUR KNEE
OFF OUR NECKS

LIVES MATTER – BRON LIVES MATTER

BLACK LIVES MATTER – EQUALITY

BUFFALO SOLDIER – BOB MARLEY

POLICE REFORM NOW

HOLD POLICE ACCOUNTABLE

Get your Knee off Our Necks – Photo –

FILIPINO FOR – NO JUSTICE NO PEACE – BLACK LIVES MATTER

DEFUND THE NYPD

DISARM, DEFUND, DISMANTLE

FREDERICK MONDERSON

FUCK THE POLICE

WHY DID YOU PUT ON THAT BADGE?

JUSTICE, PROTECTION, REPARATION
FOR BLACK AMERICANS

DECORATED U.S. ARMY VETERAN
FROM "A SHITHOLE COUNTRY"

REPEAL 50 A – BLACK LIVES MATTER
NO JUSTICE, NO PEACE

ACAB

YOU CAN'T BE ANTI-RIOT AND
CELEBRATE PRIDE MONTH DUMBASS
- # BLM – TONY MCCADE

INVEST IN PEOPLE NOT PUNISHMENT

DEMAND EQUAL JUSTICE

GET YOUR KNEE
OFF OUR NECKS

DON'T SIT BACK AND BE SILENT – SAY THEIR NAMES – BLACK LIVES MATTER

END WHITE SUPREMACY

WE ARE IN DISTRESS

JUSTICE FOR GEORGE FLOYD – REVOLT

Get your Knee off Our Necks – Photo – DON'T BE DENSE, GET OFF THE FENCE – BLM

FREDERICK MONDERSON

FREEDOM FOR ONLY A FEW IS NOT
FREEDOM

SHUT IT DOWN

BLACK TRANS LIVES MATTER

LIBERTY AND JUSTICE FOR ALL

MINNEAPOLIS TO NEW YORK – GET
AMERICA OFF OUR NECKS

NO GOING BACK TO NORMAL – NO
GOING BACK AT ALL

FELLOW WHITE PEOPLE WE MUST
NOT REMAIN SILENT

DISMANTLE SYSTEMIC RACISM

WHITE SILENCE = DEATH

JUSTICE FOR BREONNA

MAMA

GET YOUR KNEE
OFF OUR NECKS

JEWS FOR BLACK LIVES

NO PRISONS – NO POLICE

STUDENTS AGAINST RUDY CREW

DEMOCRACY FOR ALL

POLICE BRUTLITY – SASHAY AWAY

ONE LOVE – HEAR ME PLAY

DENORMALIZE WHITE SUPREMACY

I AM MY ANCESTORS WILDEST DREAMS

FREDERICK MONDERSON

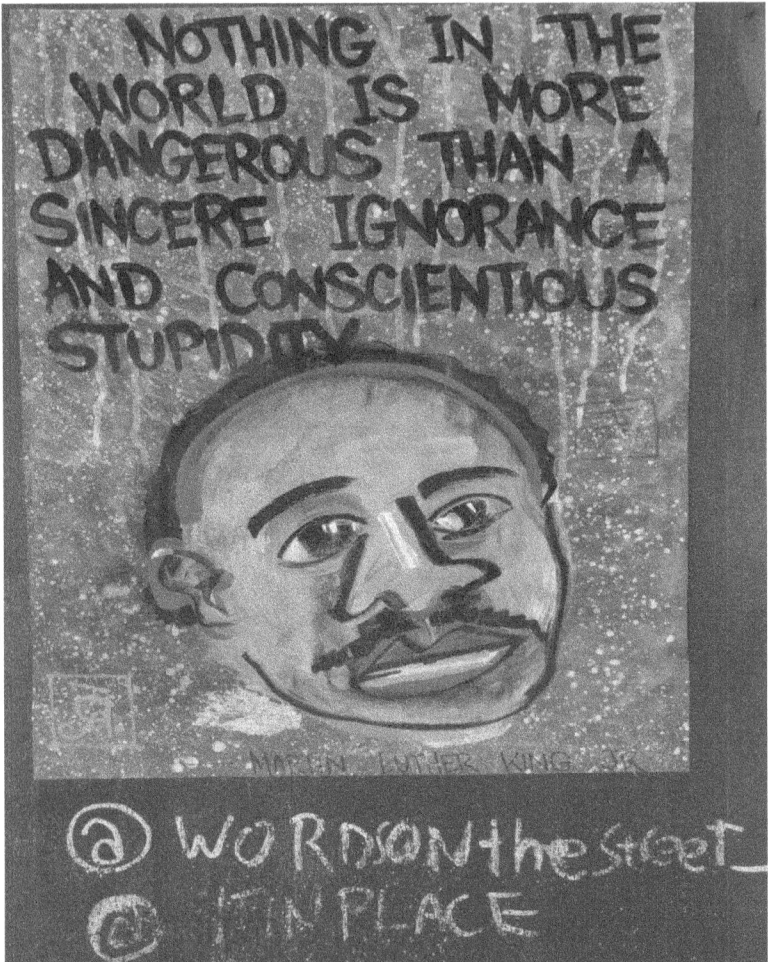

Get your Knee off Our Necks – Photo – BLM – WHERE IS OUR PRESIDENT # BUNKER BITCH

RACISM IN AMERICA TEARING APART THE BLACK FAMILY FOR 400 PLUS YEARS

GET YOUR KNEE
OFF OUR NECKS

LIBERTY AND JUSTICE FOR ALL

UNLESS SOMEONE LIKE YOU CARES A WHOLE AWFUL LOT, NOTHING IS GOING TO GET BETTER – IT'S NOT. Dr. SEUSS – THE LORAX

BLACK LIVES ARE VERY PRECIOS – GEORGE AND BREONNA WERE WORTH THE WHOLE WORLD

CONGRESS PLEASE VOTE JUSTICE IN POLICING ACT

USE YOUR BREATH, REGISTER TO VOTE

CLERGY ARE ESSENTIAL

JUSTICE FOR LAYLEEN POLANCO XTRAVAGANZA

I MARCH FOR KAWASKI TRAWIC – BORN 7-20-86 – DEATH BY NYPD 4-1-19

FREDERICK MONDERSON

Get your Knee off Our Necks – Photo –

THE WORLD IS WATCHIG

WHITE SUPREMACY IS NOT A SHARK, IT IS THE WATER

BREONNA TAYLOR'S MURDERERS HAVE NOT BEEN CHARGED

DEFUND THE NYPD – SERVICES FOR HOMELESSNESS, HOUSING, YOUTH AND COMMUNITY, HEALTH AND

GET YOUR KNEE
OFF OUR NECKS

HOSPITALS, PARKS AND REC - $5,309,929,000

MYPD OPERATING BUDGET = $5,668,823,000

ENOUGH IS ENOUGH

BLM, BWLM, BTLM VOTE

I OWE MY RIGHTS TO BLACK TRANS WOMEN

BLACK LIVES, BLACK TRANS LIVES MATTER

I CAN'T BREATHE

FREDERICK MONDERSON

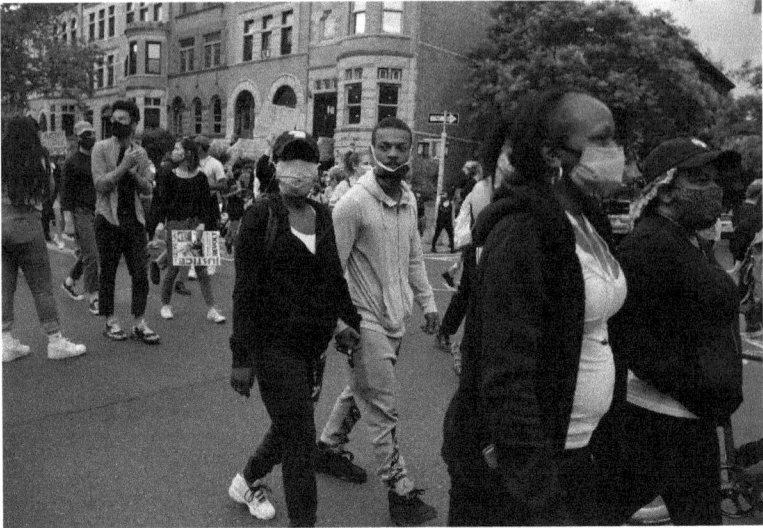

Get your Knee off Our Necks – Photo –

MINORITIES IN SOLIDARITY

STOP MURDERING FAMILY MEMBERS – DEFUND NYPD – BLACK LIVES MATTER

NO JUSTICE NO PEACE, NO RACIST POLICE

SILENCE IS COMPLIANCE

JUSTICE FOR DECYNTHIA CLEMENTS – BLACK LIVES MATTER

GET YOUR KNEE
OFF OUR NECKS

SAY THEIR NAMES

ALL LIVES CAN'T MATTER UNTIL BLACK LIVES MATTER

RACISM IS NOT GETTING WORSE, ITS GETTING FILMED

Get your Knee off Our Necks – Photo –

FREDERICK MONDERSON

DEFEND BLACK LIVES – DEFUND THE POLICE

THE POLICE IN THE MISSION LIKE THE KU KLUX KLAN

JUSTICE FOR ONE IS NOT JUSTICE FOR ALL

LATIN STANDS WITH BLM

WE JUST WANT TO BREATHE

ECHOES OF OUR PAST

NUH JUSTICE – NUH BLOODCLATT PEACE

WHO DO WE CALL WHEN THE MURDERER WEARS A BADGE?

TEAR DOWN WHITE SUPREMACY, BUILD UP BLACK PROSPERITY

DO IT FOR THE FUTURE

GET YOUR KNEE
OFF OUR NECKS

Get your Knee off Our Necks – Photo –

I'M HERE FOR THE MELANATED MOMS OF MURDERED SON AND DAUGHTERS – SEAN BELL – ANTHONY BAEZ – ERIC GARNER – KIMANI – AMADOU DIALLO – DEFUND NYPD

LET'S CARE ABOUT EACH OTHER

I AM AYANA JONES

SAY NO TO RACISM – I AM BLACK – BLACK LIVES MATTER

FREDERICK MONDERSON

MALCOLM, HARRIET, MARTIN –
BLACK LIVES MATTER - MORE THAN
A TREND, MORE THAN A HASHTAG

POLICING IS A VIOLENT ANTI-BLACK
SETTLER INSTITUTION THAT
ORIGINATED AS SLAVE PATROLS.

WE JUST WANT TO BREATHE

MY GRANDFATHER, MY FATHER, AND
I DID NOT SERVE OUR COUNTRY FOR
OUR COUNTRY TO MURDER OUR
PEOPLE

NO JUSTICE NO PEACE, NO RACIST
POLICE

GET YOUR KNEE
OFF OUR NECKS

Get your Knee off Our Necks – Photo –

JUSTICE, EQUALITY

**IF ALL LIVES MATTER, THEN BLACK
LIVES DO MATTER**

IN SOLIDARITY

FUND COMMUNITIES NOT JAILS

**IT AINT WHERE YOU'RE FROM, ITS
WHERE YOU'R AT**

FREDERICK MONDERSON

WHAT THE MIND DOESN'T UNDERSTAND IT WORSHIPS OR FEARS

IF YOU AINT ANGRY, YOU AINT PAYING ATTENTION

EITHER AMERICA WILL DESTROY IGNORANCE OR IGNORANCE WILL DESTROY THE UNITED STATES

NOTHING IN THE WORLD IS MORE DANGEROUS THAN A SINCERE IGNORANCE AND CONSCIENTIOUS STUPIDITY

Get your Knee off Our Necks – Photo –

GET YOUR KNEE
OFF OUR NECKS

I UNDERSTAND, I WILL NEVER UNDERSTAND BUT, I STAND WITH YOU – BLM

ALL LIVES CAN'T MATTER UNTIL BLACK LIVES MATTER

WHITE SILENCE EQUALS DEATH

TO BE SILENT IS TO BE COMPLICIT

SLAVERY AMERIKKK ORIGINAL SIN NEWVER ENDED, IT EVOLVED

I UNDERSTAND

WE ARE IN IDSTRESS

NOT ONE MORE

END POLICE BRUTALITY AND WHITE SUPREMACY – WE KNEEL AND WITH BLM

MAMA

FREDERICK MONDERSON

SKITTLES, ICED TEA AND A HOODIE

PROTECT PEOPLE NOT POLICE

NO MORE

WHO THE HELL ARE YOU SERVING OR PROTECTING?

CHANGE THE SYSTEM

OUR LIVES BEGIN TO END THE DAY WE BECOME SILENT ABOUT THINGS THAT MATTER – MLK

NYPD THE WHOLE WORLD IS WATCHING

JUSTICE FOR BIG FLOYD.COM

COPS ARE DANGEROUS

RESPECT EXISTENCE OR EXPECT RESISTANCE

GET YOUR KNEE
OFF OUR NECKS

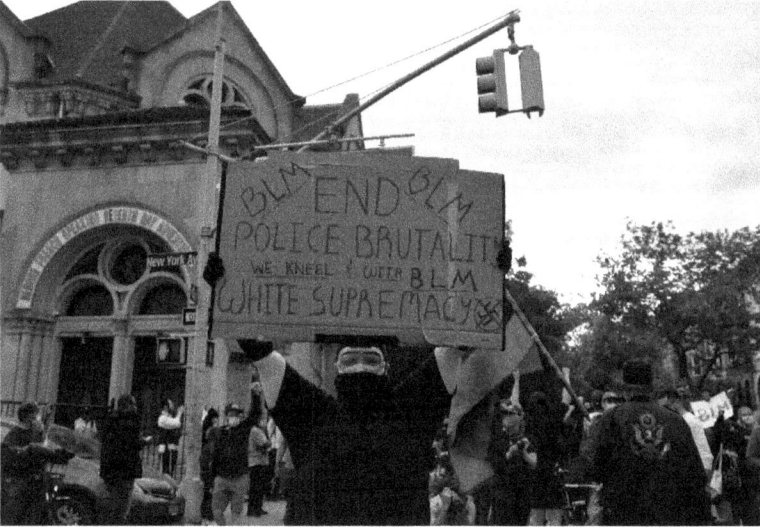

Get your Knee off Our Necks – Photo –

BLACK LIVES MATTER – WE WILL NOT STAY SILENT

FIRE DEBLASIO

WHEN WE REVOLT ITS NOT FOR A PARTICULAR CULTURE. WE REVOLT SIMPLY BECAUSE FOR MANY REASONS, WE CAN NO LONGER BREATHE – FRANTZ FANON

TO IGNORE EVIL IS TO BE COMPLICIT IN IT – MLK

FREDERICK MONDERSON

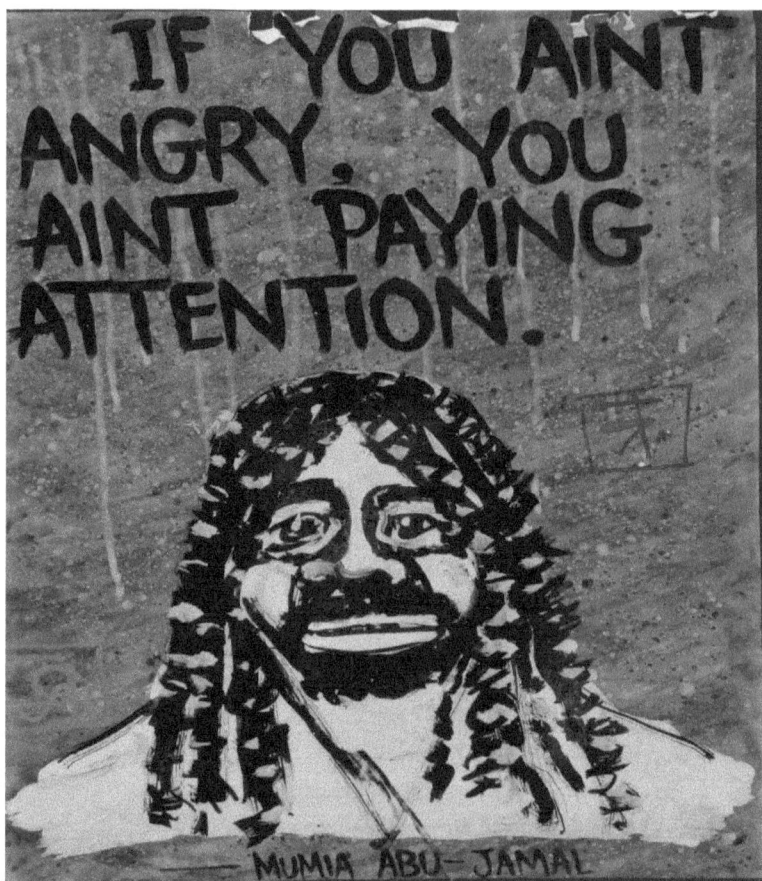

Get your Knee off Our Necks – Photo –

BLACK LIVES MATTER – TRAYVON MARTIN

WHITE GAYS OWE EVERYTHING TO BLACK LIVES

SOLIDARITY IS NOT ENOUGH

GET YOUR KNEE OFF OUR NECKS

13.   LIBERATE! LIBERATE! LIBERATE! THE WHITE HOUSE BY DR. FRED MONDERSON

Arrogance is costly; immediately to the victim and later to the victimizer! Over an extended period of time arrogance can result in political, psychological, emotional and most certainly injurious harm. The American Revolution was sparked as a result of King George's arrogance, insensitivity and contempt for the Colonists. The Declaration of Independence defined such actions as "a long train of abuse" and therefore, justification for the American Revolution and therefore justification for the American revolt that formed the new nation from the shackles of tyranny. The "Age of Trump," from campaign through Administration has been a nightmare as Donald Trump's pompous behavior is not that of a public servant but of such insidious severity, he has earned the title of "Equal Opportunity Abuser!" The ramifications of such, as David Gergen often pointed out, is "beneath the dignity of the Office of the President of the United States."

Former President Bill Clinton often referenced the might and power of the American nation is not in its military but essentially in its compassion and humanity, its big-heartedness. Power manifested in

FREDERICK MONDERSON

Donald Trump's actions is perennial abuse of men and women against whom he acts as if they are "chewing gum beneath his shoes." This is not the American way; certainly not from the pinnacle of strength represented in steadfast humility, empathy, concern and care for the least among us. Nonetheless, in his recent unchecked expressions, using his "Twitter Feed," Mr. Trump has called upon his "supporters," to Liberate Michigan; Liberate Minnesota; Liberate Virginia; states led by Democratic governors who, because of the present pandemic crisis, have followed guidelines he recommended. Other states, led by Republican governors that were forced to enact somewhat similar measures to combat the Carona-Virus, did not come in for the same call to mutiny by Mr. Trump. So much so, Governor Jay Inslee of Washington state; in response, explained, such calls for liberation, essentially fermenting revolution is "illegal and dangerous." Calls to liberate these states, a day after Mr. Trump instructed governors to "call your own shots" is a "refusal to show leadership" that "entails people to disobey the law." Even further and saying he is "extremely disappointed," Governor Inslee called Mr. Trump's actions "willfully malicious" and "dangerously bombastic dog-whistles to his base."

GET YOUR KNEE
OFF OUR NECKS

Get your Knee off Our Necks – Photo –

Amidst his spewed mayhem, Mr. Trump seems to have a latent hatred for Barack Obama as even at Coronavirus Briefings. Four years into his presidency, Trump still continues to evoke the former president's name rather than atone for the 42 million unemployed Americans now out of work, the 130,000 Corona-virus death mostly within a four-month period during the month of February 2020 in which he stalled. Added to this, the 20,000 lies and false statements he had made thus far in his term, is a truism, as Mr. Trump has stated, "Only I" can rack up those enormous though horrible numbers. Speculation would entail, Mr. Trump was probably golfing outdoors through most of this and indoors during the crisis, and so is out of touch. We know he doesn't read the Presidential Daily

Briefings on Intelligence but he chose to dominate the Carona-Virus Briefings, acting and treating it as a political campaign, seeming to imply he cares more about re-election than the suffering and deaths now plaguing the nation.

Now, much of this has happened in a few months, and if a we add the mountains of malarkey, he has manufactured over the last four years, his tenure certainly meets the criteria of "a long train of abuse" and as such, presents the need to Liberate the White House.

Get your Knee off Our Necks – Photo –

GET YOUR KNEE OFF OUR NECKS

14.   AMERICA IN CRISIS – TRUMP!

BY
DR. FRED MONDERSON

America is in Crisis – Health-wise, economic, physically, and socially though sadly but realistically we're all in this together. That is, with the exception of one man, Donald Trump, the President of the United States. Mr. Trump is not at the tip of the spear leading the charge against the pandemic malady, encouraging the American people to delve into the sphere of challenge and death. In fact, he is "leading from behind" the podium of the White House Coronavirus daily briefing as he campaigns for the fall election.

The problem with this is, he comes off as silly, insidious, shaky, mean-spirited and selfish in a sort of "while America burns, I must protect my presidency and be re-elected to the post that belongs to me" mentality. That is, instead of vigorously and effectively leading the nation, Mr. Trump is simply covering his ass now and for the future.

When, in the campaign, Mr. Trump boasted, "I can shoot someone on 5th Avenue and not lose a single vote," everyone laughed it off. Some thought it silly. When the New York Mayor Bill De Blasio announced plans to paint **Black Lives Matter** on 5th Avenue in front of Trump Towers, the President thought this idea criminal and embarrassing. When he announced he would shoot someone on Fifth avenue and not lose a vote, though this would be considered murder, it did not upset him. Now, on Mr. Trump's "watch" nearly 130,000 Americans have died in the Coronavirus-Covid-19 Pandemic during his presidency and his is not being held accountable. As leader of the "free world" and Chief Executive of the United states of America, Mr. Trump continuously shifts responsibility for problem issues to the various states while claiming credit for any positive developments that occur. This "axle-grease not Vaseline" slick trickster, even in such states, uses the term "We" for the White House when things go bad for the "only I" fault line. That is, "We when its bad or controversial; I when its good!" Sadly, this is the man who wants to be given the opportunity to lead this great nation again.

In the fourth year of his presidency, after some 20,000 lies and false statements earning the appellation of "equal opportunity abuser," failure as a leader, inciter of unethical even threatening behavior, being praised by right wing racist, peddling racist and divisive dribble, many times accused of misogynistic behavior, and much more, even demonstrating a pathological craving or covetousness for the presidency; yet, he does not see that position as a privilege or honor but rather as a right. All this notwithstanding, the American people

GET YOUR KNEE
OFF OUR NECKS

are very savvy, perceptive and can easily recognize a "con" and a "con man!"

Today, the nation is bleeding from the scourge of the Pandemic's economic and death woes, rather than demonstrate exemplar leadership, demonstrating empathy towards a bleeding nation, Mr. Trump is behaving erratic and more concerned about his re-election. In a matter of months, Mr. Trump has fired four Inspector Generals. These were Michael Atkinson of the Intelligence Committee; Mitch Behm – Transportation; Glenn Fine – Transportation Department; Christi Grimm – Health and Human Services.

We know of his right to fire but its something more. When Mr. Trump dismisses subordinates with such rapidity, many of these he terms "Obama holdovers" but these are patriotic Americans whose oath and responsibilities are about uncovering wrongdoing in the public service oftentimes, the Inspector General and Attorney generals uncover or are pursuing irregular or illegal behaviors of Mr. Trump or his associates' misbehaviors.

FREDERICK MONDERSON

Get your Knee off Our Necks – Photo –

For all he supposedly knows, Mr. Trump does not really realize, the more he attacks Mr. Obama, the more he exposes himself, his underbelly, his racism, his nervousness, his fears. Americans and the world keep tabs and dismisses him as erratic, self-serving and clownish.

GET YOUR KNEE
OFF OUR NECKS

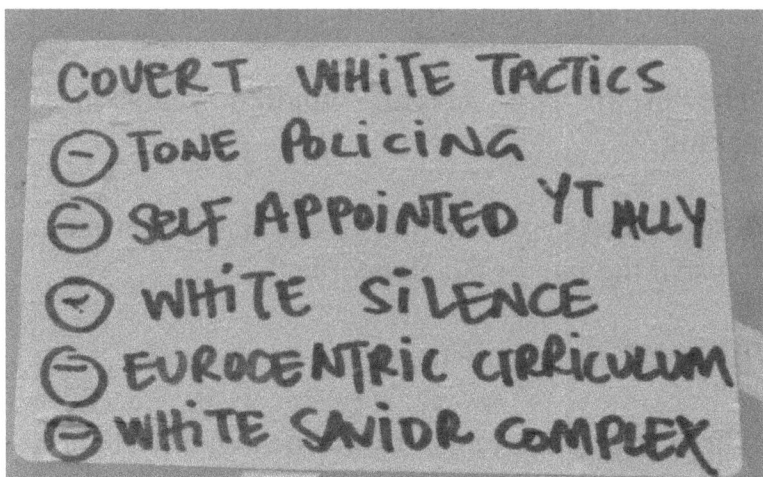

COVERT WHITE TACTICS
⊖ TONE POLICING
⊖ SELF APPOINTED YT ALLY
⊘ WHITE SILENCE
⊖ EUROCENTRIC CURRICULUM
⊖ WHITE SAVIOR COMPLEX

Get your Knee off Our Necks – Photo –

15. BLACK INCARCERATION

THE SENTENCING PROJECT –

"Blacks are ten times more likely to be incarcerated than whites."

"A disproportionate percent of Blacks is in prison."

"Race plays a role in sentencing and incarceration."

"Racial profiling is a serious problem."

"The cash bail system affects Black people."

FREDERICK MONDERSON

"We're calling on legislators and people in decision making to look at this tragedy and do something."

"The problem is several hundred years in the making."

"Racist stereotypes and biases are significant factors that seal the fate of Black people."

"We must investigate the police agencies."

"There are great racial disparities in this national institutional system."

"Police excessive use of force must stop. There must be accountability to stop abuses."

Get your Knee off Our Necks – Photo –

GET YOUR KNEE OFF OUR NECKS

16. "GET THAT SON OF A BITCH OUTTA THERE, YOU'RE FIRED! YOU'RE FIRED!" DONALD
BY
DR. FRED MONDERSON

There is always the need to be careful of what one says for it can come back to be used against the speaker. President Donald Trump coined the phrase when he railed against Colin Kaepernick, the **NFL** Quarterback who "Took a Knee" during the playing of the National Anthem at the game in effort to protest police brutality and their killing of black men and women. In the rise of his popularity, Mr. Trump at rallies depicting men and women in red outfits and wearing MAGA hats, the epitome of arrogance and bombast became the order of the day. Mr. Trump's ego projected an air of false invincibility that influenced clones to engage in acts that even threatened public safety. Again, and falsely claiming divine approval as if he was, "The chosen one," Mr. Trump began spewing the most vile rhetoric calling the media "Enemy of the people," attacking everyone who expressed views antithetical to his, firing subordinates who did not kneel and kiss his ring as Wall Street rose rapidly and unemployment declined rapidly.

FREDERICK MONDERSON

Get your Knee off Our Necks – Photo –

17. HOW DO YOU MEASURE "INCOMPETENCE" MR. PRESIDENT? BY DR. FRED MONDERSON

After former President Obama criticized President Donald Trump, calling his COVID-19 response an "absolute chaotic disaster," in his rebuttal, Mr. Trump described his predecessor as "grossly incompetent." "Elder Wisdom" classed this as "The Pot calling the Kettle Black;" the cliché messaging, nonetheless, is mute since Trump is white and Obama Black! However, on a more serious note, if we compare the two Presidents, while "absolute chaotic disaster" resulted in an enormous casualty rate in the America, from physical, financial or economic issues; the term "incompetence" has to be measured or judged through visible behavior with demonstrated impact and particularly in this case on the times, the office and on the American nation. For instance, as an example, if the first significant bill   the president passes was not Lilly Ledbetter but an enormous tax cut benefitting the wealthy, some would consider this "incompetence!"

On the one hand, President Barack Obama inherited a nation in psychological, social even emotional and economic crisis with unemployment numbers high, housing foreclosures running rampant, Wall Street wallowing in crisis, widespread bank failures that threatened financial institutions at home and abroad, as the auto industry rapidly lost market share with local and state governments experiencing significant revenue shortfall. In addition, teachers as well as police, fire and other first responders' jobs stood tottering on firing blocks.   Conversely, in bank bailouts and loans to the auto industry as well as innovations in clean energy initiatives even the first African-American President shepherd in sustainable recovery, demonstrated growth and pointed the nation towards a brighter future that he inherited. In addition, through bold and immense leadership practices, Mr. Obama creatively challenged the moral, psychological, economic and financial maladies that threatened the nation with impending failed-state status. All this, while Republicans such as Mitch McConnell, Chuck Grassley, Jim DeMint, Joe Wilson, in concert with some 20 Republican heads of NGOs vigorously attacked President Obama and the Affordable Care Act, maliciously labeled "Obamacare." Yet, despite these pernicious and orchestrated obstacles and odds, Mr. Obama persevered and handed his successor, Donald Trump, an economy structured on a solid foundation with the image of America greatly restored from the "go it alone" attitude demonstrated in the post-9/11 Iraqi invasion that toppled Sadam Hussein.

However, while not acknowledging Mr. Obama's successes, in braggadocio fashion, Mr. Trump was able to finesse the economic and financial policies Mr. Obama put in place and then claim he was the architect for the alarming rise on the stock market and lowering of the unemployment rates. In that self-praise fashion, he pointed to the thousands of men and women in red outfits who attended his political rallies cheering him on while ignoring his degradation of the Office of the Presidency. He downplays the ever-expanding pandemic sweeping across the various states.

GET YOUR KNEE
OFF OUR NECKS

Get your Knee off Our Necks – Photo –

How ironic, Donald Trump, a person who rose to political success by villainizing and victimizing Mr. Obama in the most horrendous and racist manner; yet, benefitted tremendously from Mr. Obama's successes in the many areas pointed out above. Even more significant, Mr. Obama was successful in securing America's leadership role in the Paris Climate Accord. He successfully pivoted to the Pacific in the Trans-Pacific Partnership (TPP) agreement seeking to tamper China's rising influence and its threats to American and her allies' interests. In the painstakingly worked out Iranian Nuclear Deal, Mr. Obama blunted that nation's gallop towards nuclear armaments; and in his withdrawal from this agreement Mr. Trump removed any restraints on Iran's nuclear and other geopolitical ambitions that were in place. In poor leadership and shameful imitation of Obama's decimation of Osama bin Laden, the terror mastermind, Donald Trump assassination of an Iranian general resulted in an Iranian barrage that wounded nearly one hundred American soldiers further resulting in Iran registering an arrest warrant with Interpol for Donald Trump, the American President. This may sound bizarre but it's a fact. Nevertheless, and, most certainly, President Obama gained the respect of America's allies particularly through charm, his infectious smile and his effective leadership style. These many accomplishments Mr. Trump rescinded, withdrawing the nation from global participation in the above-mentioned important issues and developments. Much more significant, as leader of the "free World," Mr. Trump should have been at the head of these many tables. However, his ineffective leadership cost the nation prominence in such developments. How embarrassing it is for Americans to be barred from entering Europe due to President Trump's failed leadership on the Carona-Virus Pandemic.

GET YOUR KNEE
OFF OUR NECKS

Get your Knee off Our Necks – Photo –

All this notwithstanding, in final analysis and for these many years after leaving office, Mr. Obama is considered one of the most, if not the most, well-liked and respected men, political leaders, icons, on the face of the earth. Significantly, in an "age of numbers," Mr. Trump may have invoked Barack Obama's name perhaps 1000 times since his arrival. As such, commentators need to know, 'Is it envy or racism or both?' Equally too, given the criticism and Mr. Trump's supposed future, the new accusations against Mr. Obama, unfounded as they are, this is just another attempt to deflect from the President's woes and failed leadership now glaringly exposed in a pathological craving to be re-elected to a second-term he hardly deserves, and many argue is the "captivity of the American Presidency." Let's not forget, Ambassador John Bolton determined, "Donald Trump is unfit for the Office of the Presidency."

GET YOUR KNEE
OFF OUR NECKS

Get your Knee off Our Necks – Photo –

It is clear, Donald Trump came in bubbling with an arrogance and bombast; insulted people left and right; behaved too confident displaying his now revealed obnoxious personality; told more than 20,000 lies or false statements; then he shamefully began undercutting Obama, railed against his many achievements included pursuing an unrelenting hatred against the ACA, and overturning the former president's many international agreements with little to show for such arrogance. In rescinding or withdrawing from the many international agreements Mr. Trump opened the door for America's enemies to get a foot into the door or a seat at the table while pursuing their own nefarious interests. Now, with the Coronavirus pandemic malady, Obama is the only voice sounding an alarm, given Republicans have been silenced, resulting in Mr. Trump essentially "sleeping at the leadership wheel" evident in the "absolute chaotic disaster" syndrome.

Let's face it. It's not so much what you say but what you do. Anyone who makes more than 20,000 lies or false statements and does not know or believe they are such, despite what the world acknowledge based on fact checking, then that person is an "absolute incompetent." If one has to use force to get compliance and support as "Trump holds Republicans captive demanding loyalty," or be consigned to the dungeons of failed re-election, then that is not genuine leadership. It needs be recognized; such actions are not genuine leadership but are grounded in a pathological insanity which is beyond incompetence. It is sad, while Mr. Trump's followers view him as "Golden," other see him as

GET YOUR KNEE
OFF OUR NECKS

mere "cosmetic" and this reflects on their mis-
understanding of reality which matches his
alternative reality. Andy Slav ill accused Mr. Trump
of 3 failures. (1) Failure to provide moral leadership;
(2) Failure to adapt to changing circumstances; (3)
The failure of empathy or imagination. This critique
equally applies to Republicans in Congress who turn
a blind eye on Trump's egregious and erratic
behavior, fearful he would instruct his followers
against their reelection. Recent developments show
a Republican group has endorsed Joe Biden for
President because they believe their party leader is a
threat to the nation's security and well-being.
American wisdom holds, "Anyone who does not
stand for something, will fall for anything" and so
many "lost" Americans are following this Pied Piper
over the cliff of social reality and historical scrutiny,
all of which will ultimately have deleterious effects
and impact on their time of living, service and
name, given leadership seems uncaring about these
individuals futures. This is indeed "incompetence" a
Donald Trump character flaw.

FREDERICK MONDERSON

Get your Knee off Our Necks – Photo –

18. TO GRADUATING CLASS OF 2020

"We're all in this together."

"Reach for the stars; Never give up on your dreams."

"Relish in that, go out there and make change. Change the world, but change humanity." Anthony Anderson

"The light bulb went off. Drive, motivation to be successful. I am going to drive, not away from my community but to benefit my community." Keith Wallach.

GET YOUR KNEE
OFF OUR NECKS

"Smart. Fearless. Some people see things as they are; some people wonder; some people carry the ball over the goal-line." Keegan-Michael Key.

"We're so proud of you." Mark Foster.

"Don't let society limit what you can do! Push yourself."

"One of the biggest accomplishments of my life. I don't remember a damn thing about my graduation. You are the 'Class of the pandemic.' Put in time, effort, read books, do the things that are meaningful. In this, character, intellect and being human counts." Jason Alexander.

"We love you Class of 2020."

"We honor friends, family, community. Thank you. You should be proud. You made the sacrifice. The Class of 2020 is going to be something special. We're ready for you to change the world." Lebron James.

"I'm a Senior."

"Everything just changed.
What do we do now?
We are still Seniors.
It's still our moment.
It wasn't a year we expected."

FREDERICK MONDERSON

"There are 3.7 million High school Seniors this year."

"O Say Can you see American Anthem

Black National Anthem

"What makes a Senior?
Every moment from the day you are born to this moment.

Sponge Bob - School Bus
Middle School - U-tube - A New Era

We were made for this. We will not be defeated. We were born to make noise." Zen Daya

Get your Knee off Our Necks – Photo –

GET YOUR KNEE
OFF OUR NECKS

"I'm falling.
Hope I'm not the only one. Are you falling?
I'm falling in love with the one who will break my heart." Dua Lip

Priscilla Arceru – High School Valedictorian. First in family to get a degree. What she did for me was not seen at first. We can create projects of excellence."

"When we get knocked down, we get up stronger. We did it together."

"We will be safe.
Vote – Red, White and Blue.

"I love giving air hugs.
Love you. Honor my teachers. Thank you, teachers."

The Black Box Theater –

Every Generation has a defining moment.
An indelible experience.
Come together
Benefits, hindsight
Demand better together.

Who makes your decisions?

Themes of trial and triumphs. Take the torch and lead your movement."

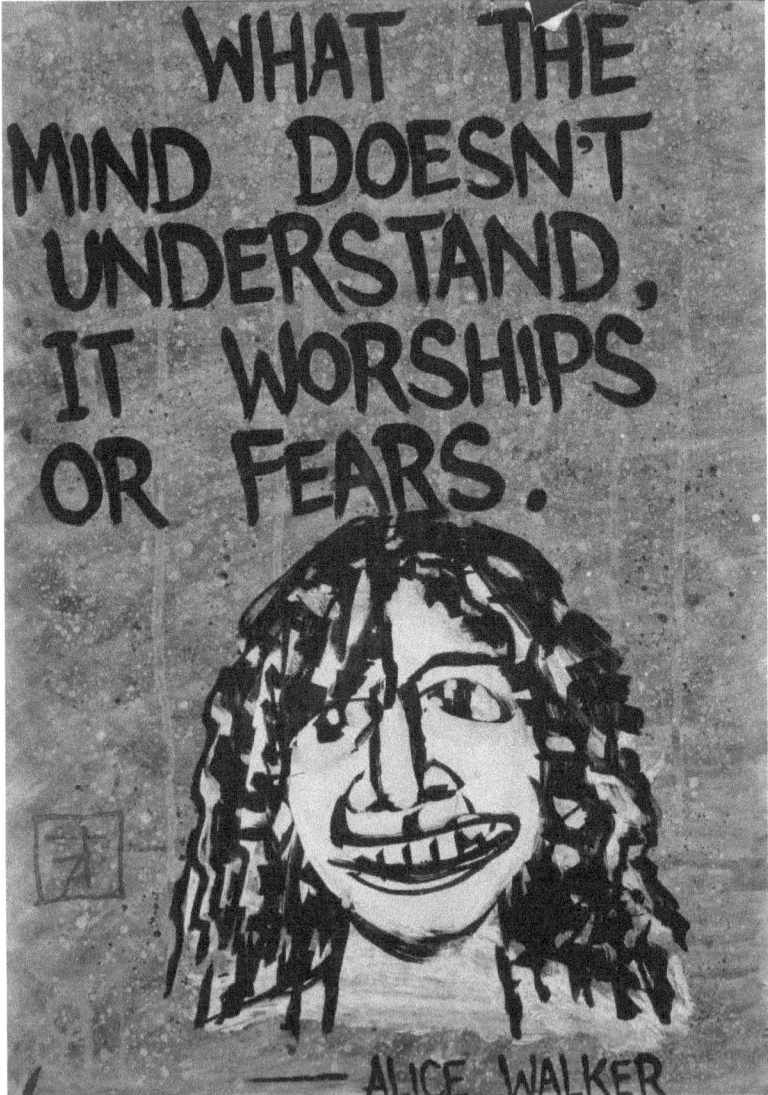

Get your Knee off Our Necks – Photo –

The Platt Brothers –

GET YOUR KNEE
OFF OUR NECKS

"Here's to the Ones.
Memories bring back memories."

"It's been a long day my friend,
When I see you again."
Vermont High School

"Stay strong, give thanks.
The most important thing is to have respect for others."

"Try new things. Water your plants.
Learn from others not like you
Love you man!"

"Many girls will be forced into early marriages and low paying jobs.
The world is your and what you make of it." Malala

"Use your voice to live and learn."
Lena Waithe

"Shiny
Ain't nobody gonna take my crown
Gonna make it."
Chika and B-Mike

"Hooray for Jordan.
She taught me how to eat better.
To be the sexiest guy around."
Skak

FREDERICK MONDERSON

Get your Knee off Our Necks – Photo –

"We can come together in incredible ways.
Creativity, resilience, humility. There is no such
thing as too much education."

"Sometimes
You have those feelings out of place." H.E.R.

"We are family.
They say we won't make it."

"It's a critical role schools play in our lives.
Support
Protect
Feed
Safety Net

GET YOUR KNEE
OFF OUR NECKS

Teachers, coaches, parents
Time to go to your new life's work

Promise to your communities

Rectory, churches, schools,
Build your future

My message is to stay clear sighted to become
excellent in every endeavor
Explore every possibility
Go as far as you can
You're all Kings and Queens
Lebron James.

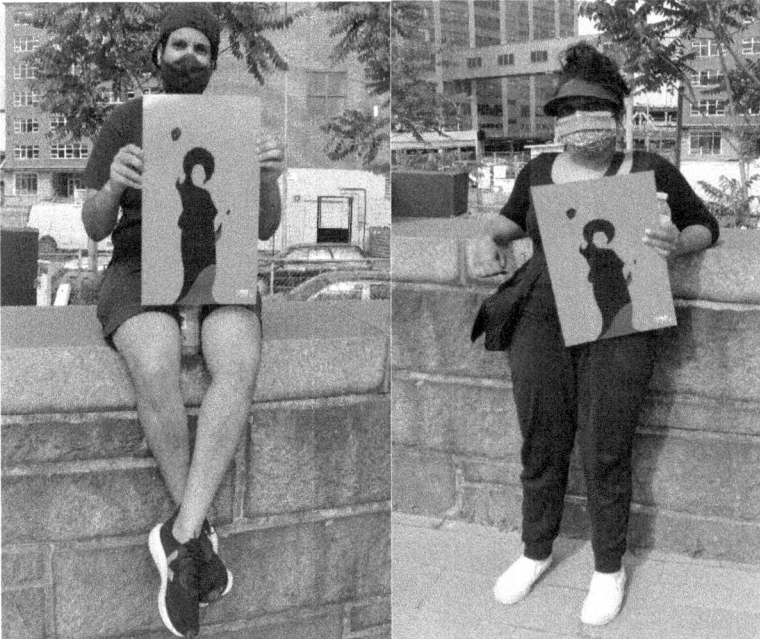

Get your Knee off Our Necks – Photo –

FREDERICK MONDERSON

"When we exercise and display energy, imagination, tenacity, nothing matters. You will give the world more power."
Henry Winkler

"This has been a memorable achievement.
You must fail many times before you succeed."
Juan Soto of the Washington Nationals.

"Congrats. Baby, you did it! You're resilient. That is commendable." Kalen Allen.

"Congrats! Parents, Educators, Friends.
We face an uncertain future.
Embrace the challenge.
The world and country need you
It's your future
Our planet that's at risk.

Take care of the sick.
Go on with your lives
Celebrate what we have in common.
Dignity and mental respect.

Overcome challenges only if we chose to face them.
Unite not divide
Build not tear down.
Your example will inspire the world
Class of 2020 will rise to heal the divide. Bill C.

GET YOUR KNEE
OFF OUR NECKS

"Born in 2001 and Graduate in Pandemic."

Get your Knee off Our Necks – Photo –

"Be open to experiences as best as you can.
Keep an open mind.
Billions of people on the planet but only one you.
People who changed the world did it differently.
Sarah Blakely.

Get your Knee off Our Necks – Photo –

19.   BEN, BILL AND DON!
BY
DR. FRED MONDERSON

What a trio! Ben Carson, William Barr and Donald Trump. These are not the "Three Stooges but the highest-ranking government officials in the land. They do, however, have problems with the truth, statements, even interpretation of data.   More important, additionally they are comfortably snug in

GET YOUR KNEE OFF OUR NECKS

a three-seater vehicle driving in the wrong direction on the superhighway of history. Notwithstanding, destiny sometimes affords persons the opportunity to write, put a mark upon the pages of history with the most long-lasting impact on human memory. While top of the mountain status demand top of the mountain behaviors, in terms of communication, empathy, humane behaviors, efforts to ensure justice and equality; basically, it insists treat others as you would want to be treated. Most important, display of trust and integrity in human relations helps guard the solemnity of one's name; so, in the future one's persona will be either honored or dishonored based on the severity of related displays.

Dr. Benjamin Carson was well-respected in the Black community for his "Gifted hands" as a great neuro-surgeon. However, somehow, along the journey he lost his way, being baited by "30 pieces of silver." In earning that approbation, he became a Poster Child for the Heritage Foundation, an institution that likes Black the least. No less significant, Mr. Carson's "Greatest hit" was his attack on Barack Obama's Affordable Care Act by unabashedly stating, "Obamacare is worse than slavery!" Imagine, a law that helped 50 million American who lacked Health Care is under perennial assault. The audacity of this Black man to attack the first African-American President whom Jessie Jackson, on the day of his first Inauguration, explained, "Barack Obama is the best the Civil Rights Movement could provide." That is to say, the ship on which Dr. Carson sails is so laden with racists, KKK, white supremacists, Alt right, etc., all anti-Black, at least perhaps one, if not more, will consider Dr. Carson "A Nigger," as Ted Nugent despicably labeled Barack Obama, "The Nigger in the White House." Still, Carson may say "I'm not a Nigger," perhaps "Honorable White." Though his Republican cohorts think otherwise!

Bill Barr had the spotlight shine on him when he wrote a position paper essentially placing President Trump above the law. As the position of Attorney General became vacant in as much as Jeff Sessions reclused himself from the Muller Investigation in process, this infuriated Mr. Trump. Given Mr. Barr's "White paper," the President nominated him to fill the position. How history repeats itself for Mr. Barr was previously Attorney General and he defended President George Walker Bush, Number 41, in a similar situation many found questionable.

None-the-less, again, as the Muller Investigation unfolded and this coincided with Mr. Barr's Senate Confirmation hearing, his pledge to be neutrally objective, despite his record in defense of Mr. Bush and the White Paper, he was confirmed as Attorney General. Then the Muller Report was released and while it remained silent on "Conspiracy between the Trump campaign and Russia," it did not exonerate him of "Obstruction of Justice."

GET YOUR KNEE
OFF OUR NECKS

The Attorney general hastily called a press conference (mis)interpreting the Muller Report favoring the President and this act generated a great deal of blowback wherein one commentator remarked, "Mr. Barr's credibility is now in the gutter." Time and time again, Mr. Barr defended the President's questionable actions, words, lies, etc. So much so, House Speaker Nancy Pelosi labeled Mr. Barr not the nation's top law-enforcement attorney, Attorney General, but "Mr. Trump's lawyer." Such behaviors have caused persons as David Macatee to remark, "District Attorney Barr's corruption is in defense of President Trump," while Andrew McCabe, former Deputy FBI Director spoke of his "confusion and incompetence." And that Mr. Barr's actions are responsible for "misrepresentations that undermine the confidence in the Justice Department."

Donald Trump assumed the Presidency he should not have won; yet, he embarked on a cavalcade of insults and lies that mushroomed into two clouds, one took pride in kissing his ring while the other sought to kick those who objected. Like any virus or plague that spreads unchecked, Mr. Trump's lawlessness and abuse from Allies to Zambia, whether in lies, name calling, threats, inciting unconscionable actions, even encouraging KKK, Nazi, racists and white supremacists to emerge from beneath their rocks mired in offensive goo.

FREDERICK MONDERSON

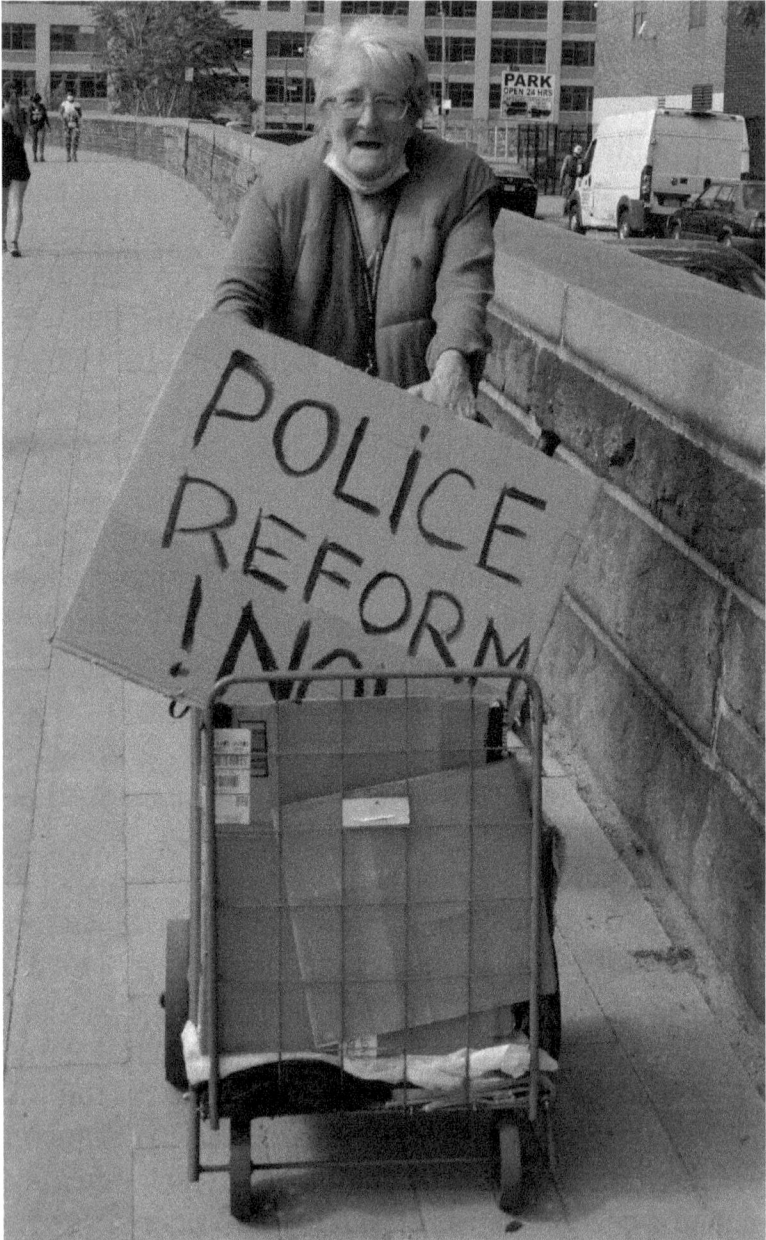

Get your Knee off Our Necks – Photo –

GET YOUR KNEE
OFF OUR NECKS

From the citadel of Olympus, weak leadership, lack of accountability for any and all acts, thoughts, tweets, etc., emanating therefrom emboldened Mr. Trump's followers, associates, campaign personnel, even appointed government officials, all mirroring that motley crew who signed up to attack Rock Ridge in the movie **Blazing Saddles**., to accept any behavior or perpetuate such. Like a flood, cascading across the American landscape a mindset emerged that "People don't believe Donald Trump," and "Most Americans believe Donald Trump is dishonest." We know he is a liar as former Secretary of State, that great Republican 4-star General Colin Powell publicly acclaimed on CNN's State of the Union, "He lies!" Interesting how his response to Mr. Powell's condemnation fell so flat. It's like being in a crowd and going into a corner to squeeze out some foul air and trying not to be too offensive. After all, Powell once affirmed, my position as Secretary of State is temporary, but "I'll always be a General." And so, he was joined with other top generals, Jim Mattis, John Kelly, General Dempsey, General McMaster, General Allen and Admiral Craven who informed the nation from their exceptional viewpoint, among other things, Mr. Trump embarrassed the nation, demonstrated weak leadership, insulted too many people and is indeed a pathological liar and a threat to the national interest. As all this happened, the George Floyd murder happened. In so many respects, President Trump's inflammatory behavior in response was like "pouring gasoline on a fire." In this regard,

FREDERICK MONDERSON

Representative Pramila Jayapal accused Mr. Trump of "racist, xenophobic hate-filled behavior." In concert with Attorney General Bill Barr, she spoke of political interference particularly in the Roger Stone case and in exasperation felt "fear of the president's corruption."

Get your Knee off Our Necks – Photo –

The marked ghastly nature of the murder of George Floyd so infuriated the American people, even the entire world, their action represented an overflow and cascading of behaviors rejecting the plague of racism, inhumanity and institutional inequality underscored by Mr. Trump's unchecked and unapologetic arrogance that instigated an uprising in the streets from one end of the nation to another. As protests mounted in city after city, an unthinkable occurrence transpired. Citizens converged in

GET YOUR KNEE
OFF OUR NECKS

Lafayette Park in front of the White House, the People's House, Donald Trump's temporary sojourn, and the next unconscionable act saw them dispersed with tear gas, pepper spray, rubber bullets and a mass of uniformed law and military forces, in storm trooper fashion, demonstrating their might against the peaceful protester. As they dispersed and the smoke cleared, Mr. Trump emerged ahead of top members of his inner circle and walked towards St. John Episcopal Church. Mr. trump, ahead of these enablers, stood on this "Holy Ground," then raised and brandishing a Bible, inadvertently turned upside, not choosing to open it or praying, posed for a photo op. This heartless blasphemy so infuriated the truly religious community, they condemned the President's action in the sternest and most unimaginable manner.

Apparently, *The New York Times* newspaper reported Mr. Trump saw the crowd and descended into the White House bunker, taking his wife and son. First, Mr. Trump condemned *The Times* article, emphasizing is his earlier claim it was "fake news," simply stating he went down into the bunker "to inspect it." Then to rehabilitate his false claim to "tough guy statue," the American citizens, in front of the White House, the prerogative to exercise the cherished constitutional right to peacefully protest be damned, his "Storm Troopers" could be observed mercilessly wading into everyone there.

FREDERICK MONDERSON

As Mr. Trump stood on religious grounds making a mockery of his false and blasphemous claim to be "the chosen one," flies in the face of divine acknowledgement.

Get your Knee off Our Necks – Photo –

So, we have "Rub a Dub, three men in a tub," exhibiting behaviors full of dishonesty, deceit, and decadent distrust. Thus, as today's reality manifested, many American institutions, finally coming around, have admitted "There is systemic racism across the American landscape." Yet, Mr. Carson, Mr. Barr and even the President refuse to admit such is the case. The depth of racism in this country, percolating for four hundred years against the Black man so stained and ingrained in the American psyche it can't even be "white washed."

GET YOUR KNEE
OFF OUR NECKS

Now, Mr. Kudlow, the president's economic adviser, has joined the threesome making it a "Gang of Four" wo insists "There is no institutional racism in America." Such a claim flies in the face of millions in the American streets and worldwide protesting and affirming "Justice for George Floyd," "Black Lives Matter," "We Want Peace Not Patience," hoping "A Change is Gonna Come!" Yes, it will!

Get your Knee off Our Necks – Photo –

20. LAMAR, LAMAR, LAMAR
BY
DR. FRED MONDERSON

Retiring at the end of this term, he will become a former Senator, Lamar Alexander, it is not "Bernie or Warren" you must worry about, it is former President Barack Obama. To recall, as the Impeachment of President Trump conducted in the senate and final results hung in the balance with the world watching and you considered a paragon of balanced virtue and perhaps you yourself gave the impression you would be fair and impartially objective, many stood in heightened expectation. Alas, in giving your "Thumbs down" decision to at least sow independence, fairness and weigh in on right and truth, you purportedly stated, "Though Democrats made their case," Donald Trump and his judges must be acquitted for such is better than "Bernie and Warren." Thus, your decision crushed truth and justice like an enormous weight leaving untold numbers of mouths ajar. Perhaps you never realized Edmund Burke wrote, "The only thing necessary for Evil to triumph is for good men to say or do nothing!" As such, in this instance and by Mr. Burke's yardstick" you are not a good man and evil has indeed triumphed as a result of your decision. Remember, you admitted, "Democrats made their case" and as a trusted member of the "world's most respected deliberative body," you drove your vehicle down the wrong direction on the

220

superhighway of history. In essence, Senator Alexander, you voted against truth, justice, righteousness, philosophic and practical ideals of integrity and morality that for long characterized the truly outstanding American personality. In ancient Egypt, this social and philosophic admonition was called **Ma'at**. Its antithesis is **Isfit**, the word for evil, on whose side you have chosen to cast your vote as you retire.

Much has been said about President Trump's control of and reshaping of the Republican Party, his threat to "unleash his base" against any party member who do not toe his line and so, "Mum's the word!" The few Republicans with "grapefruits for nuts," who spoke against the President's questionable actions and words did not seek re-election for fear of "The Wrath of Con!" Mr. Conway and his group, who have stood-up always spoke truth to power, and so are the exception to the rule. In essence, the others have stained their political career for in silence there is complicity and this may end their elected political career on a sour note. You, for the most part, had an opportunity to join that rare and exceptional breed of outspoken elected Republicans but sadly you chose to be saddled with the negativity associated with an ill-considered decision.

FREDERICK MONDERSON

Get your Knee off Our Necks – Photo –

On Tuesday April 14th, former President Obama endorsed his former Vice-President Joe Biden for President in the 2020 election. In contrast, to President Obama and your leader Donald Trump, there is not comparison. How sad, you could not be on the right side of history.

Men in leadership roles chose to follow leaders of a higher disposition of proven courage, integrity, analytic ability, honesty, truthfulness, perception, empathy, humility and vision that, spot on, can inspire others. The man you owe allegiance to, Donald Trump possesses none of these virtues. Barack Obama, on the other hand, does possess a great deal of these attributes, being a man of

GET YOUR KNEE
OFF OUR NECKS

elegance of mind and nobility of spirit. Just as "Being like Mike," men the world over love, respect and wished to be "like Obama." Women too. For example, Barack Obama was mobbed in Germany asking he become its president and in England he floored them, while "Mighty Michelle," in photograph seen hugging the Queen an unheard-of reality, Queen Elizabeth invited her to "Come back for tea." On the other hand, the British people asked Mr. Trump to "hurry up and leave," and in same manner owing to his mismanagement of America's Carona-Virus response, the European Union has barred him and Americans from entering Europe, the home of the Western Alliance your man leads. How tragic, and this can be counted as part of your legacy! Adding misery to virus, Iran issued an arrest warrant through **INTERPOL** for President Trump!

Your choice of **Isfit over Ma'at** is not surprising. Your longevity in the Senate and equally in as much as top echelon Republicans conspired against that great American President, Barack Hussein Obama, it stands to reason you stood with your party unalterably opposed to this first African-American Chief Executive. David Stockman, former budget Director of President Ronald Reagan often admonished, "Where you sit is where you stand, and where you stand is where you sit." That you are an American Senator is not an indictment; that the world waited in amazed anticipation of your vote and not unexpectedly you favored Donald Trump, history will remember you in the most unfavorable manner.

Get your Knee off Our Necks – Photo –

In that Senate Impeachment trial of President Trump, when one of the House Managers acted somewhat inappropriately, Chief Justice John Thomas reminded all participants, they were in the "world greatest deliberative body." Therefore, you Sir, are or were among that great of body of thinkers and the world looked to you for wisdom and you proved wanting in ignoring the many shortfalls Mr. Trump demonstrated in the present captivity of the American Presidency.

GET YOUR KNEE
OFF OUR NECKS

21. MURDER OF GEORGE FLOYD

GLORIA BROWN-MARSHALL –
"Constitutional Professor at John Jay College of Criminal Justice - "The system failed George Floyd on every level."

She quoted W.E.B. DuBois "The system was designed to fail Blacks from the beginning."

BENJAMIN CRUMP – Attorney at Law – "We are seeking Justice for the United States and George Floyd is the best example I have seen to reach this ideal for this nation."

"When we fight for the 'George Floyds' of the world, we fight for America to live up to its creed."

MELISSA MURRAY – Law Professor at New York University School of Law - "Which part of the Video America has not seen before."

"It's time for us to stand up and say enough is enough."

FREDERICK MONDERSON

REV. JESSE JACKSON – Civil Rights activist and American icon – "We need policy change."

REV. AL SHARPTON – Civil rights Activist - "We don't want no favors, just get up off of us.

"We couldn't breathe, not because there's something wrong with our lungs, but because you have your knee on our necks."

"We won't stop. We'll keep going until we change the whole system."

BENJAMIN CRUMP – Attorney for the Floyd family, appearing on Jim Sciutto's **CNN** program made the following comments in response to the Impact George Floyd's death has had on unfolding events. He stated:

GET YOUR KNEE
OFF OUR NECKS

Get your Knee off Our Necks – Photo –

1.   The Minneapolis City Council has voted to replace the local Police Department.

2.   Congress has passed the George Floyd Justice and Policing Act. The family is relieved. However, there is still need for systematic reform. Partisan politics at this time of challenge is worrisome.

3.   Now is the time to avoid delay. The momentum generated by citizen outrage may fade. This is different as young people say time for change is ripe.

4.   Politicians are warned, do something now or come November, you will be out of a job.

5.   Minnesota and other states as Georgia, Alabama, are passing legislation in the name of George Floyd.   However, we must get to the national level.

6.   People who saw the video are motivated to have laws that bring change.

THEOLONIUS FLOYD – Testifying in Congress insisted – "I will not let his death be in vain. Make sure his death is not in vain."

"We loved him and the world loved him."

"This is the first time we have the chance to change the culture and behavior in America."
"This is our time! This is our time!"

"Stop the pain. Listen to the call for police reform."

IKRAN MOHAMED – "We know that all of the injustices against African-Americans have been present beyond what has been caught on camera."

MARIO GRANT – "I've been so angry and upset this past week, but mostly tired of it all."

AYU GEMEDA – "I'm here so that 20 years from now, we are not seeing history constantly repeat itself."

GET YOUR KNEE
OFF OUR NECKS

NICOLE SULLIVAN – "We all feel very burdened not just only by the death of George Floyd, but just by the oppression in the country and the systemic racism."

Get your Knee off Our Necks – Photo –

22.   THE SCOURGE OF RACIAL
HATRED
BY
DR. FRED MONDERSON

FREDERICK MONDERSON

As a student of the esteemed Professor Dr. Leonard James at New York City Technical College of the City University of New York, Brooklyn, among hundreds, perhaps thousands, we were taught a Methodology of History very different from the usual. Not foremost the question of when something happened but what happened, how it happened, why it happened and last but not least, when it happened. There were also other variables such as the ability to make Critical Comparative Historical Analyses and the role such factors as Internal and External developments play in creating outcomes that are favorable or unfavorable.

One such ingredient as part of the Methodology of Historical Evolution, Internal and External, can be applied to a discussion of the question of racism in America, today an issue many believe needs attention but never gets. Many will agree, decisions of great significance need a point, place or time of departure in order to arrive at a satisfactory conclusion or answer to the question under study. In that case, the External and Internal components of the Methodology can be applied to the phenomenon of recent events in Charleston, South Carolina. Interesting, the tragedy of Charleston raised the issue of "heritage" and its dynamics as manifested in history, hate and racism. Of significance, purported harmony among citizens, while in fact, deep-seated racism simmers beneath a sheer veneer full of ugly puss, and if pricked can easily explode.

GET YOUR KNEE
OFF OUR NECKS

That is to say, heritage should truly be considered on both sides of the racial equation.

Sad to say, the Mother Emanuel Charleston Church martyrs proved a catalyst and drove a number of subsequent developments to the surface, chief of which were the viciousness of the church massacre with intent to incite a race war; the realization, even a "holy place" is not immune from such violence; a profound and true belief in the goodness of God and the forgiving nature of the "victims;" the bold and courageous vision to recognize the existence of prevalent racism and hatred masquerading as heritage and the actions to speak out against such harmful negativity; a realization, removal of the Confederate Flag was not only easy but soothing; and most important, this entire phenomena is only the "tip of the Iceberg," and must be urgently addressed to help America shed the shackles of this devastating psychological ball and chain that stifles its moral compass especially in all its prevalence across the South.

Strange, but this boiling cauldron is not really new and can be easily traced in a series of developments emerging, sadly, from as late as 2008, even if we, in this respect not give much attention to the previous age through which the foundation of all this rests. From the time Barack Obama declared for the Presidency, in 2008, the scab of American racism was pricked and slowly but profoundly it began oozing the puss of a sin that has long stained the conscience of this nation. Winning the Presidency, all manner of opposition declared in response to a Black man leading the nation, itself in jeopardy of falling into failed-state status from which he gloriously rescued his beloved nation. From militias who began arming to the teeth for a race war fabricated in their own minds and belabored to impressionable youth and seasoned racists alike; to Dylann Roof following in this putrid path seven years later who massacred in and stained a holy place, which was actually a race-war misfiring dud, unable to spark the mischievous intent; and from an Arizona pastor who prayed for Barack Obama's death to "Daddy Cruz" who wanted to "Send Obama back to Kenya," but when Obama offered him Cuba he declined. Then we had Mitch McConnell who failed to "Make Obama a one-term president" and "Waterloo DeMint" who surrendered his seat, to "You Lie" Wilson and "Stupid" Grassley who could only languish while Obama won twice in the Supreme Court. We could only conclude across that wide spectrum of anti-Obama and anti-Black sentiments many "South Carolina Flag" defenders "hate" and "racism" stand camouflaged in business suits across the nation, drenched in perfumes to cover the stench of the racial hatred they harbor, such as that expressed by Ole Papi who instructed, "Don't re-Nig!" If restful sleep is a clear conscience, these are all insomniacs!

In the 2012 Presidential Election all the Southern or "Lynching" states voted for Mitch Romney but ostensibly they voted against the Black guy. These slaves owning Confederate or rebel states could not countenance, given their history, of being on a Black man's plantation. However, it was more than that and it can be argued, the unforgiving nature of losing the Civil War, giving birth to the Ku Klux Klan ideology and practices of lynching as exemplified in the Memorial display of the Equal J justice Initiative in Montgomery, Alabama and the books they published that documented some 4004 southern lynchings of Black men to which terrorism of Black folk, denial of due process and the right to vote and hold office in a climate of Jim Crow and separate and unequal, having discrimination and terror as its hallmarks, reflect a fiery hatred not easily quenched even with the passage of time. Hence, the hatred and racism the South Carolina legislators identified in association with the Confederate flag Governor Haley finally removed is a well-camouflaged fact abounding denials, notwithstanding.

Given that ideas and practices masked as beliefs and heritage are extremely difficult to surrender and given all of the above, and the fact a good man such as Mr. Obama could not win a Southern state, then the "Carolina Syndrome" is effectively masked and deep seated as especially represented in the 2012 vote.

Recently *The New York Times* featured an article about the Southern legal eagle who documented some 4,004 lynchings and racial killings across much of this nation's southern landmass from 1877 to 1850. This area, sad to say, is hard hit by the Carona-virus pandemic and still, many are praying for their recovery.

The gentleman vowed to memorialize these "Heritage Sites" with a marker. Equally, and given that such cultural markers will blemish a lily-white topography, resistance in the "Carolina Confederate Mold" is expected but the nation must confront the problem.

Granted some business entities have raised the issue of divesting from states publicly promoting the "Confederate Brand," the first and most profound question that arises becomes, "Is this an economic epiphany or a moral obligation?" If the first, then it is a strategic decision to forestall the consequences of an economic boycott of such a state. If the latter, it is a realization on the part of some to divest of the racial albatross this baggage of heritage brings at a time when the consequences exert a stiff penalty in moral and material payments. Second, "With slave trade and slavery, 19th Century racial terrorism and 20th Century lynchings among other unspeakable acts, do residents who live in the potential marker site states have the courage, strength, conviction and wisdom to forgive, themselves, for that history of unspeakable acts?"

GET YOUR KNEE
OFF OUR NECKS

Therefore, still more questions can be posed, given the legacy of slavery and resistance and the prevalence of a Confederate culture across the South, which after all, was a defense of slavery. Thus, the first question is, "Must there be another horrendous act before hate loses?" Rodney King asked pointedly, "Can we all get along?" Should the old legacy of hatred, terrorism and racism remain in the chest and trotted out ever-so-often? The contradiction is, young people want a united country with equality for all given there are so many, internally and externally, who envy and plot against the goodness of this nation as represented by the forgiving nature of the victims of the Charleston Massacre who refused to be chained to the burdens of tit-for-tat hatred.

The irony is, this is a praying nation so "Do we have the courage to confront the malady" allowing the force to change to emanate from within our Christian values and institutions? "Can we truly teach multiculturalism in our schools?" "How do our practices and teachings affect the young who long for a tranquil future undergirded in truth?" To address the myriad problems, we must move beyond and address the inequality that has plagued our nation for the longest. That is rich over poor; white over black; man over woman; war hawks over peace doves; rural versus urban; employed and unemployed for as Lincoln admonished, "A house divided against itself cannot stand." It should not be only when catastrophe strikes do the nation come together for a minute.

Americans are thought to be able to do anything but "Can these physicians heal themselves?"

Then again, contrary to misguided beliefs that though Africans are a god-fearing, praying and forgiving people, we are by no means cowards. Aristotle made the contradictory mistake in ancient times when in his work **Physiognomonica** he declared "Egyptians and Ethiopians are cowards because they are black!" What the great scientist did do, first is affirm the ancient Egyptians and Ethiopians were Black Africans. Second, and unfortunately, he misjudged the martial prowess of the Back man evident from the many wars they fought down through the ages.

Internecine warfare for the burgeoning wealth of the Nile Valley; Old Kingdom pharaohs represented as smiting the Bedouin at Serabit el Khadem; Mentuhotep II pacifying and uniting the land to establish the Middle Kingdom; Senusert establishing his boundary at Egypt's southern border in Nubia during the 12th Dynasty; Sekenenra-Ra unleashing a protracted 50-year war of liberation in the 17th Dynasty and his sons Kamose and Ahmose expelling the Hyksos, finally founding the 18th Dynasty and New Kingdom. Whether Amenhotep I, Thutmose I's efforts or Thutmose III's brilliant military strategy on the Plains of Megiddo; Rameses

GET YOUR KNEE
OFF OUR NECKS

II dominating at Kadesh; Merenptah, "My country, right or wrong;" Rameses III against the "Peoples of the Sea;" the Ethiopians Khasta, Piankhi, Shabaka, Shabataka and Taharka at Thebes and in Palestine, all happening before "Alexander the Great." Then there was Hamilcar, Hasdrubal and Hannibal Barca challenging the Roman Empire; the Haitians at the Revolutionary War Battle of Savannah; the Buffalo Soldiers on the American Plains; Samori Toure against the French in West Africa; Yaa Asantewaa against the British in Ghana; Shaka Zulu against the Boers in South Africa; and one could ask the Italians about their defeat the Battle of Adowa in 1896 at the hands of Menelik II. Let us not forget Blaise Diagne recruiting 100,000 West Africans to stem German obliteration of French Manhood in World War I; Black Americans Charging up San Juan Hill protecting Teddy Roosevelt's Rough Riders and Black Americans overseas fighting "to save the world for democracy." Haile Selaisse stood against the Second Italian coming; the Tuskegee Airmen fought brilliantly in World War III; the feared Black soldier in Vietnam and our boys in the Gulf, Afghanistan and Iraq are remarkable examples of modern military prowess. We cannot also forget the thousands of Black Veterans buried in the Brooklyn Navy Yard including Samuel Carson who died in the Mexican War and in being repatriated to Ghana, West Africa, opened the "Door of Return" so long closed instead of the "Door of No Return" dating back centuries.

Thus, the malicious should know, while Alack Americans would rather pray than fight, all should understand when fighting becomes a last resort, then it is. Many look to Giovani Machiavelli who admonished, "Any man who wishes to make a profession of Goodness must naturally come to grips with many who are not good. Thus, he must learn how to be good and not good and use and not use this knowledge as the situation warrants."

Therefore, Americans must girdle themselves in a forging mold reminiscent of the "Charleston martyrs' families" and work for the betterment of the nation, not their narrow racially motivated and stained self-interest. In every respect, the old labor movement's admonition "United We Stand, Divided We Fall" should be our watchword as we face the future particularly in view of the many futuristic policies and practices put in place by President Obama. That is, we should not be guided by divisive racist tropes, no matter who is in the White house.

GET YOUR KNEE
OFF OUR NECKS

Get your Knee off Our Necks – Photo –

23.　COMMENTARY ON
DONALD TRUMP – THE MAN

JOHN BOLTON – "Hopefully we can repair the damage of one term, I'm not sure we can with two."

"I tried to portray an accurate picture of what went on."

"Donald Trump has put profit and greed ahead of the country."

"The Democrats committed impeachment malpractice."

"I wrote this book for history."

"He's worried the American people would see the book."

"My conscience is clear."

"There is a thing the President says in public and more in private."

"By taking this to the Senate and failed, Democrats empowered the President."

"Our adversaries are taking notes on our Corona-virus response."

MARCO RUBIO – "Everybody should wear a damn mask!"

ANTHONY FAUCI – "Get past it. It is not a political but a public health issue."

BEN JEALOUS – "Donald Trump will be a racist to the end."

JIM SCIUTTO – "Donald Trump has put his interest over the nation's interest."

GET YOUR KNEE
OFF OUR NECKS

Get your Knee off Our Necks – Photo –

GLORIA BORGIA – "Everything is about the election."

"Scary."

"In Trump's world, there is confusion, lack of systematic philosophy and consistency."

"He has turned a blind eye to the truth."

SECRETARY OF STATE MIKE POMPEO – "Bolton is a traitor."

JOHN HARWOOD – "Donald Trump has two issues that impacts his image going forward. That is, first: "Republicans who for nearly four years have been silent about his many and unspeakable actions."

"He is not going to change his divisive habits that focus on himself."

"He is a significant underdog not just on the national stage but in the battleground states."

DAN RATHER – "We want to believe he cares."

"Its all about him and his re-election."

STEVE ADLER – MAYOR OF AUSTIN, TEXAS – "Our hospitals will be overrun by mid-July."

"We're receiving mixed messages."

RON NIRENBERG – MAYOR OF SAN ANTONIO, TEXAS – "We're receiving mixed messages like mask wearing."

GENERAL MICHAEL HAYDEN – "I don't know what the President is trying to do."

"I don't know what is the solution to what he is trying to do."

GET YOUR KNEE
OFF OUR NECKS

Get your Knee off Our Necks – Photo –

GENERAL JAMES CLAPPER – "Bolton's book represents an inside baseball perspective."

"The White House has basically given up on the Pandemic."

"I'm concerned about the election."

"American institutions are under assault by the Attorney General himself."

FREDERICK MONDERSON

ELIE HORNUG – "Bill Barr has taken the Department of Justice to a disturbing level."

"The Department of Justice is building cases according to Donald Trump's whims.

GENERAL MILLEY – "Cohesion leads to success. Divisiveness leads to defeat."

JOHN BOLTON – "There's an empty chair in the Oval Office."

NED LAMONT – CONNECTICUT GOVERNOR – "You must self-quarantine."

PAUL ROMER – NOBLE PRIZE WINNER – "It's very puzzling that this president is opposed to testing. It's not working. It's not working and he refuses to acknowledge this. This is self-destructiveness."

DAVID GREGORY – "Donald trump is politically self-obsessed. This is irresponsible."

JARED POLIS – "At this time the need for a fair and objective investigation of police-related killing is critical."

GET YOUR KNEE
OFF OUR NECKS

Get your Knee off Our Necks – Photo –

JOSH DAWSEY – "The numbers are trending in the wrong direction."

ANDREW CUOMO – "You played politics with this virus and you lost."

"Denial is not a good strategy."

JOHN KING – "Numbers are Troubling, Troubling and more Troubling."

FREDERICK MONDERSON

Get your Knee off Our Necks – Photo –

MITCH LANDRIEU – "We know who he is. We must demonstrate who we are by going to the polls."

"We are an embarrassment on the world stage."

APRIL RYAN – "It is a slap in the face of the Black Community to hold a rally in Tulsa on Juneteenth."

WOLF BLITZER – "We need real leadership to lead us out of this crisis.

DR. SCHNAFNFER – "The time to normalize wearing masks and social distancing is now so we will be comfortable with it in the fall."

GET YOUR KNEE
OFF OUR NECKS

DAN GALLO – "People are not complying enough."

DR. CARLOS DEL RIO – "Poor messaging we're getting."

"This is a war. Our fore-parents went to war and the least we can do is wear a mask."

"In this pandemic we must wear a face mask, social distance, wash our hands and don't congregate in groups."

"We can wear a face mask and not doing so is incredibly irresponsible."

MARC MORIAL – "Trump's response to the Carona-Virus Pandemic is grossly incompetent, wobbly, weak, jerky, jerky."

"There is no confidence in his leadership and it is cold-hearted at this moment of crisis to have the Supreme Court overturn Obamacare."

"He is faced with an unprecedented set of crises and his weak leadership shows malpractice in the White House."

BILL MOYERS – "When injustice becomes law, rebellion become viral."

FREDERICK MONDERSON

"Trump loathes the media and because it built him, it can undo him."

DEREK JOHNSON – PRESIDENT NAACP – "This president has normalized racism."

"He is a racist who has normalized white supremacy from the White House."

"Donald Trump is not good for the country, not good for the globe and not good for this society."

"Steve Miller is in the White House and that's part of the problem."

"We're ready to move forward."

Get your Knee off Our Necks – Photo –

GET YOUR KNEE
OFF OUR NECKS

APRIL RYAN – "There were 150,000 Blacks who served in the Civil War and 40,000 died. Where is he on preserving lynching laws affecting the south?"

JAQUIN CASTRO – "Donald Trump is inconsistent with Texas values."

WALTER BROWN – "When President Trump sent his supporters in Michigan to liberate the statehouse, he essentially unleashed the virus and now that state is hurting in the expanding set of numbers. It is easy to understand what would have happened to Black men if they had approached the statehouse with guns. Many would not have come home alive. Trump is, however, staying silent and so are those fools."

Get your Knee off Our Necks – Photo –

KIRSTEN POWERS – "The White House is trying to avoid a topic not acceptable against the President and not amenable to his narrative. People listening to Main Stream Media are taking precautions about this virus. People listening to Right Wing Media are not taking precautions."

"Fox News is harming their viewers."

DAVID ZURAWIK – "If you wear a mask, social distance and don't get in a room with many people you have a chance."

SUSAN GLASSER – "Donald Trump is inside the Hannity bunker."

"His poll numbers are going down at an alarming rate. In a 50-minute interview with Hannity he spent 3-minutes on the virus that has killed 125,000 Americans. He is disconnected from reality."

"Not just ideology but untruths Trump and his Vice President are offering."

ANGELA RYE – "No one is surprised with Donald Trump endorsing people who shout 'White Power' ideology that exacerbates this division."

GET YOUR KNEE
OFF OUR NECKS

"We know Donald Trump is a racist. Look at how he targeted those elected Black Women, then April Ryan, called Black men Thugs, and NFL players 'Sons of bitches.'"

**Get your Knee off Our Necks –
Photo –**

JOHN BOARDMAN – "The concept of the President of the United States disseminating an image of White Power is in conflict with Mississippi removing the Confederate flag."

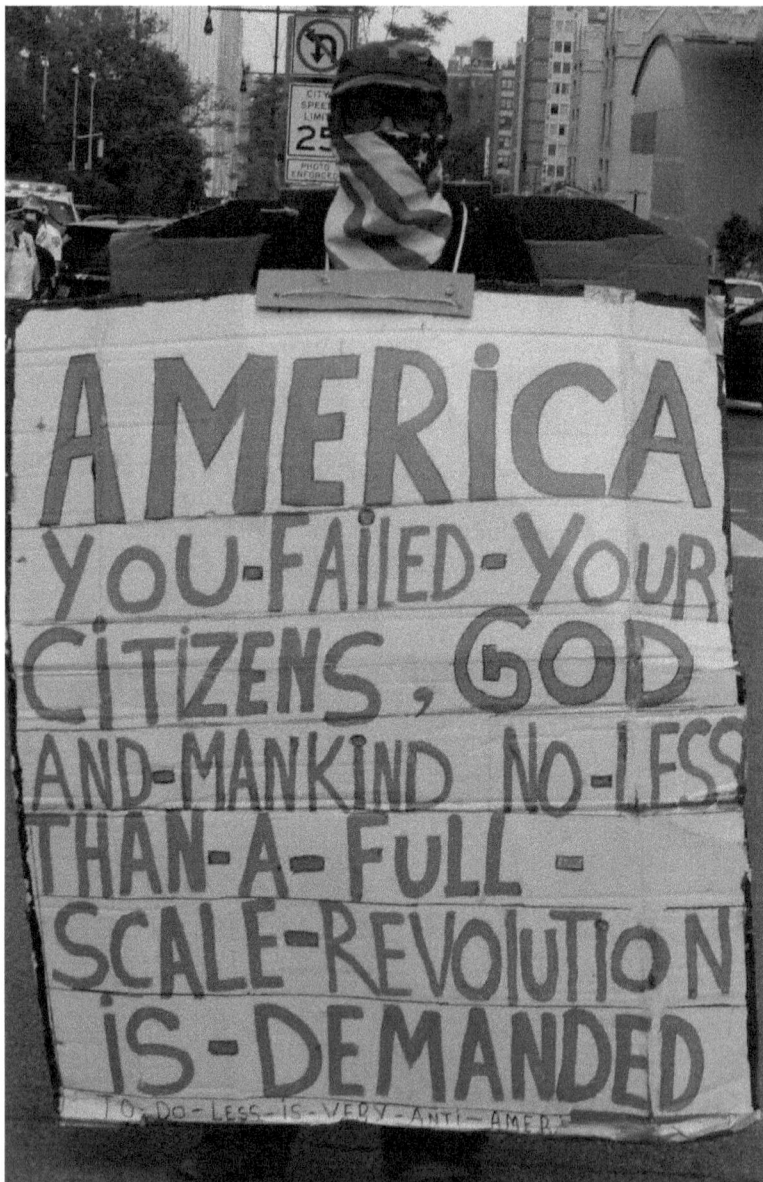

Get your Knee off Our Necks – Photo –

GET YOUR KNEE
OFF OUR NECKS

DAVID GREGORY – "Retweeting the racist trope is dangerous and the president ought to reject the call of White Power."

CARL BERNSTEIN – "Trump is a danger to the national security."

"Trump gave away the store to Erdowan in Syria."

"Putin is a Grand Master in Chess. Trump is a Sunday afternoon Checkers player. He lacks competence. He is indeed incompetent. He lacks preparation. He is only concerned with his re-election."

ABIGAIL SPANBERGER – "The President denied he was briefed about Russian Bounty on American soldiers in Afghanistan. This is highly unlikely. Russian briefing would very likely be included in the Daily Briefing."

"Several high-level Intelligence sources confirmed this intel so it would be part of the Daily Briefing. If he read it is another story. If he did not read it, then why? If he was not told, then why?"

It is "deeply worrying" that the President first took Putin's word over that of US Intel experts; He is pushing for Putin to be included among the G-8 world leaders; he wants to invite Putin to the White House, even as Intel indicates there's a bounty on soldiers and marines risking their lives while serving abroad."

CARL BERNSTEIN – "High level officials as Generals McMaster, Kelly, Tillerson and Mattis pointed out, the President is reckless, unstable, and absolutely sadistic, especially towards women. He abused Theresa May and Angela Merkel. He said Chancellor Merkel is stupid and lacked courage even that she played into Russian hands. He is irresponsible and out of control.

Someone described Trump and Putin as "Two guys in a steam bath."

MS. CORDERO – "The common thread throughout the Trump Administration is the abuse of power."

PAUL ROSENZWITZ – "The president and Barr are on the same page."

"I'm convinced, the Attorney General is a lawyer who represents Trump and not in the interest of the American people."

GET YOUR KNEE OFF OUR NECKS

Get your Knee off Our Necks – Photo –

JEFFREY TUBIN – "The Flynn case is a perfect example of Barr's abuse of power."

"Barr has politicized the Department of Justice more than anyone since the time of Richard Nixon."

CARL BERNSTEIN – "Donald Trump as a credible leader should expand Medicare, secure the ballot, establish equity for all citizens, denounce the ideology of white supremacy, and reject the separation of Americans based on race.

SUSAN RICE – "You don't flail the messenger. You accept the bad news and then get set to solve the problem."

"This President is in dereliction of duty as Commander-In-Chief regarding his troops serving in harms way."

In regards his deference to Russia, what does Putin have on him? - Regarding Donald Trump's behavior: "(1) He obstructed the Muller Report; (2) Took Putin's word over American Intelligence; (3) Withdrew US forces from Syria giving Putin an enormous advantage there; (4) He called for Russia to rejoin the G-7; (5) He wants to withdraw one third of US forces from Germany, which is a boon to Putin; (6) Now this bounty on US forces and he does nothing; (7) In addition he wants to invite Putin to the White House. This is deeply troubling to owe loyalty to a foreign government over American forces."

"All these principles need strong leadership." I will help Joe Biden to become the next President to combat the issues President Trump lacks leadership in and is in denial about."

DONNA SHALALA – "We need government. We need a strong government at the National, State and Local levels."

GET YOUR KNEE
OFF OUR NECKS

Get your Knee off Our Necks – Photo –

"We need strong leaders with courage in a moment of crisis."

"The president's inability to lead has led to Americans dying. Never thought I would Say this. This is about patriotism, lack of leadership."

LEON PANETTA – "The President has gone **AWOL** from the job of leadership."

"Rather than provide leadership on the corona virus and other such issues. He resorts to tweeting about vandalism of statues. He is not good at crises. He is in dereliction of duty."

THOMAS FRIEDMAN – "We're not leading; We're not following; we're lost!"

"We want someone who believes in science and can assess data."

WOLF BLITZER – "We need real leadership to lead us out of this crisis."

"The time to normalize wearing masks and social distancing is now so we will be comfortable with it in the fall."

DR. SCHNAFFNER – "People are not complying enough."

GET YOUR KNEE
OFF OUR NECKS

**Get your Knee off Our Necks –
Photo –**

a.   SINCE ABRAHAM LINCOLN
BY
DR. FRED MONDERSON

Accordingly, President Donald J. Trump recently announced, "I have done more for Black people than anyone since Abraham Lincoln."

Sadly, Mr. Trump believes what he is shoveling!

FREDERICK MONDERSON

Get your Knee off Our Necks – Photo –

1.   As a pathological liar, everything Mr. Trump says is either a lie, a false statement or a contradiction and sadly, he has "no regrets."

2.   Mr. Trump often insists he does not take responsibility for anything. Really, that is, he seems to take credit for anything that "Appears to be good;" but he "disowns the bad." The arrogance of this racist white man is appalling! He probably means he insulted more Blacks than anyone since Abraham Lincoln that would mean he outdid "Bull Connor," Police Chief Allen and Alabama Governor "George Wallace."

Malcolm X mentioned "Gas Oven" mentality, given contemporary climate, we have to say "Thank God for Barack Obama." That is even more important given the shallowness of the critique of those Blacks who falsely claimed "Obama was not doing enough for Black People." Seriously, the only counterweight to Donald Trump and his followers and types is Barack Obama who has been a bulwark against any outrageous action against African-

GET YOUR KNEE
OFF OUR NECKS

Americans. As many acknowledge, "Been there and done that" with its implications.

3. Again, while Mr. Trump does not accept responsibility, he certainly does accept credit as he does with the Stock Market when it goes in the upward direction and when he claims Black unemployment rate dropped under his presidency.

Sure, as the economy escalated thanks to the foundations Barack Obama put in place, white unemployment dropped and to fill the rising need, Blacks were hired to fill positions that were not first choice for his base. Many of these jobs involved brooms, mops, waiters and guards. In photo-ops on the Trump White House lawn and elsewhere, not only the proverbial "Fly in buttermilk could not be seen," for he is often surrounded with nothing but Whites even among the interns. Perhaps there was a Black or two, "Spooks" by the door for false comparison. Nevertheless, while the Blacks were the last hired, they were naturally the first fired. Now, with more than 40 million unemployed, who knows when Blacks will be hired. Perhaps, that will happen after the 96 percent vote for his reelection. However, "Mother Nature" will have some say in this.

Mr. Trump's claim is so ridiculous, bombastic, it flies in the face of reason and insults the untold numbers who have worked for and struggled to advance the cause of Black Progress.

FREDERICK MONDERSON

Get your Knee off Our Necks – Photo –

Booker T. Washington – A slave who educated himself then attended Hampton Institute. He was a staunch Pan-Africanist. He developed a profound philosophy, economic and social, forerunner to the "Do-for Self." It was called "The Tuskegee model." Tuskegee Institute founded by Booker T. Washington, trained more Blacks to be self-reliant and thereby contribute to Black upliftment, much more than Donald Trump has uttered lies and falsehoods, now well past 20,000.

Marcus Garvey – The father of Black Nationalism whose name resounds most powerfully more than 80 years after his death. He is responsible

GET YOUR KNEE
OFF OUR NECKS

for founding the Universal Negro Improvement Association and the African Communities League. Marcus Garvey established the Red, Black and Green flag that is today a philosophical and social shibboleth that galvanizes his race, wherever they are located.

W.E.B. DuBois – The first Black Harvard University PhD. He is considered one of the most brilliant theorists and successful writers of the Twentieth Century. This literary giant is the "Father of Pan-Africanism," one of the most potent political and intellectual philosophies active in the world today. In combination with the Red, Black and Green, Pan-Africanism is considered by far the philosophical Battle Theme of the **African Revolution** worldwide.

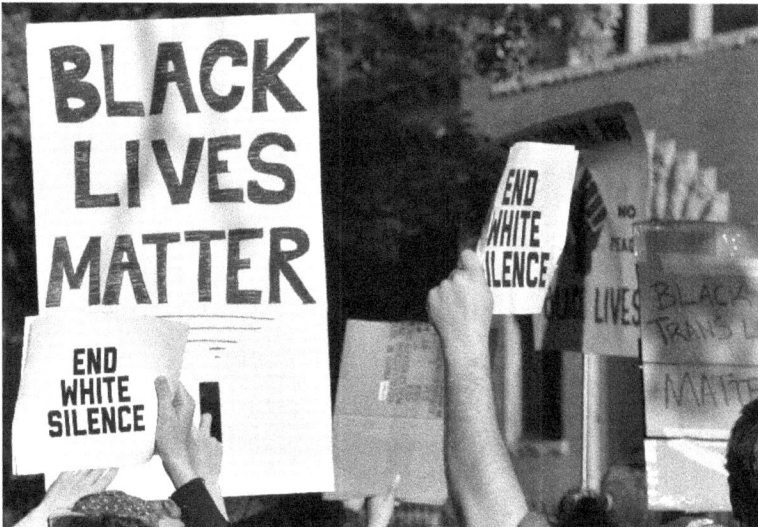

FREDERICK MONDERSON

Get your Knee off Our Necks – Photo –

Asa Randolph – President of the Sleeping Car Porters Association aboard American rail. His statue is located in the Union Rail Station in Washington, DC. He was a prolific writer and extremely active activist. He threatened to have some 50,000 Black Men gathered on the Great Lawn to protest jobs discrimination in the War Industries 1941, on eve of America entering World War II, forced President Franklin D. Roosevelt to open jobs in the nation's war industries.

Elijah Mohammed – Founder of the Nation of Islam, Black Muslims, an organization that has grown to millions of members who are essentially the most socially adjusted Black people in the United States.

Thurgood Marshall – First, he was successful overturning "The White Primary," then led the effort to desegregate the nation in *Brown v. Board of Education of Topeka, Kansas* in 1954. This brilliant legal mind was appointed to the United States Supreme Court and became one of its most outstanding jurists. Courthouses and other buildings were named after Thurgood Marshall.

GET YOUR KNEE
OFF OUR NECKS

James Baldwin – Brilliant literary mind who read all the books in his local library. He wrote masterpieces both at home and in his exile in Paris.

Dr. John Henrik Clarke – Man of vision, fortitude and foremost African "Sovereignist," who advocated African revolution, economic self-sufficiency, education as a tool on how to get and use power. Professor of African History, Dr. Clarke influenced a great many men and women who held him in the highest regard as an intellect, revolutionary thinker and Pan-Africanist.

Queen Mother Moore – Matriarch of African self-help organizations in America. As her name, Queen Mother, indicates, she has been tremendously outspoken in defense of African-American culture and has been the first woman, American, to address the Organization of African Unity in Addis Ababa. She chose Winnie Mandela to replace herself as Queen Mother of the African World.

FREDERICK MONDERSON

Get your Knee off Our Necks – Photo –

Rev. Shillingsworth – Prolific and courageous activist leader who participated extensively in the Civil Rights Movement.

Martin Luther King II – Dr. King needs no introduction. His words reached the far-corners of the world and been significantly inspirational for all forms of protest and resistance to inhumanity of man to man. His "Letter from a Birmingham Jail" is counted as one of the greatest literary expressions detailing injustice and resistance, even as a non-violent and creative protest expression.

Malcolm X – "The "Shining Black Prince" has been, despite what may be said, a great light and inspiration who spoke to the suffering of Black people with an eloquence and simplicity even the un-learned understood. Ibram Kendi regarded,

GET YOUR KNEE
OFF OUR NECKS

"Malcolm X as having the most significant influence in the consciousness and thinking of the African in America.

Medgar Evers – Civil Rights activist, murdered in his driveway at night, but he has grown larger in death and continues to be a light and inspiration as a civil rights icon.

Harry Belafonte – Singer, activist, whose melodic voice has inspired and galvanized many toiling in the field of resistance to racism and racial oppression. His songs are even played at sports events to rile up fans in support of their teams.

Kwame Ture – Formerly Stokely Carmichael, author of the book, *Black Power*, he has been an unrelenting spokesman for all people resisting tyranny, racism and he relished the struggle to express the right to vote.

FREDERICK MONDERSON

Get your Knee off Our Necks – Photo –

Barack Obama – African-American President, a man of monumental stature at home and abroad who many look to for inspiration and safety.

Rev. Al Sharpton – What more can be said about Rev. Al? Long toiling in the field of social activism, his famous phrases, "Whose Streets, Our Streets," and "No Justice, No Peace," have become symbols and rallying cries the world over, but particularly in the street protest now gripping this nation. No man's voice and words have been timelier and more effective, that is, not counting Dr. King of course.

And so many more.

The last of these, Al Sharpton is noteworthy, as stated. Long-after Donald Trump has been returned to his padded cell, the brilliance of Rev. Al will be highlighted as his works keep moving us forward. Today, his shibboleths, "Whose Streets, Our Streets;" and "No Justice, No Peace" resounds as inspiration in creative protest parades throughout the nation and across the world.

b. PRESIDENT OBAMA'S CRITIQUE BY DR. FRED MONDERSON

Realizing the stress, strains and challenges of the Office of the Presidency, particularly in troubling times as these, former presidents generally do not critique their successors; at this time though, they stand ready to offer the creative knowledge of their experience. Sadly, however, President Trump, perhaps out of paranoia, more likely hatred or envy, has refused to seek assistance from his predecessors, particularly the most recent, Barack Obama, whose name and persona Mr. Trump has perennially lambasted almost on a daily basis. Many see not simply a sign of disrespect, perhaps because Mr. Obama was the first African-American President, and there is a deep-seated pathology relating to this, but Mr. Trump represents the midnight as opposite to Mr. Obama's high noon.

Recently, George W. Bush then Barack Obama commented on the Trump Presidency. In the former case, Mr. Bush emphasized the need for unity particularly during this time of pandemic and perhaps reflecting back upon his 2005 Presidential reelection address in which he recognized and decried racism then plaguing the nation. Maybe Mr. Bush recognized racism has advanced rather than retreat under the present administration especially give Mr. Trump's attitude towards the principal African-American, former President Barack Obama, though this behavior deficit extends to others as well. In this observation, Mr. Bush further recognized the impact Mr. Trump's rhetoric, attitude and behavior has on influencing the actions of many persons who look to him as a hero, given he is the President of the United States, head of the Western Alliance and "Leader of the Free World." This, in Trump's and his minion's behaviors, represents not "The better angels" but the "worse devils," staining

GET YOUR KNEE
OFF OUR NECKS

the American character as the world watches and wonder, how American leadership has descended from the heights of a mountainous plateau to the depths of a valley.

Former President Barack Obama, on the other hand, has leveled a scathing critique of President Trump calling his handling of Mr. Trump's White House Coronavirus Covid-19 pandemic response, "an absolute chaotic disaster." The former president, speaking by audio to former administration alumni spoke in a no-holds-barred conversation saying the Covid-19 pandemic "would have been bad even with the best of governments but that of the Trump administration has been disastrous." As such, he stated further, "That's why I, by the way, am going to be spending as much time as necessary and campaigning as hard as I can for Biden." In addition, the audio recording obtained by *Yahoo News* revealed Mr. Obama also questioned Attorney General William Barr's decision to drop charges against former Trump National Security Adviser General Michael Flynn who lied to the FBI about his involvement with Russia in events surrounding the 2016 presidential election, and became a subject of the Special Counsel Robert Muller's investigation. In light of the Muller Investigation, Mr. Barr proved controversial as he had written a "White Paper" indicating the president essentially had unlimited power. Many commentators criticized Mr. Barr's report take on the Muller Report, his promises to be objective during confirmation hearings to succeed his predecessor Jeff Sessions and finally his action earning him the designation, not the people's but "Mr. Trump's lawyer."

Through much of the Muller Inquiry, Mr. Trump's behavior of "dangling pardons" to witnesses led many to question whether the President's actions were appropriate. Now, Mr. Barr's decision to drop charges against Mr. Flynn, observers argued, Mr. Trump did not have to issue a pardon in this case. Important, in this respect, Mr. Obama's critique of Attorney General Barr's actions indicating, "There is no precedent that anybody can find for someone who has been charged with perjury just getting off scot-free."

Many elders counsel the young advising, "Do not associate with unsavory characters because you will be held responsible for their actions." Sadly, Mr. Barr, who is "In too deep" is perennially being forced to defend Mr. Trump's outrageous actions. This puts Mr. Barr in a precarious position to be seriously chastised by historical commentators who recognize, "Mr. Barr is a willing fall guy" whose "Integrity is now in the gutter!" That is, while he buries his head in the legal sand, he exposes his legal rump to be scrutinized, castigated even chastised. But Mr. Barr should have known better.

GET YOUR KNEE
OFF OUR NECKS

FREDERICK MONDERSON

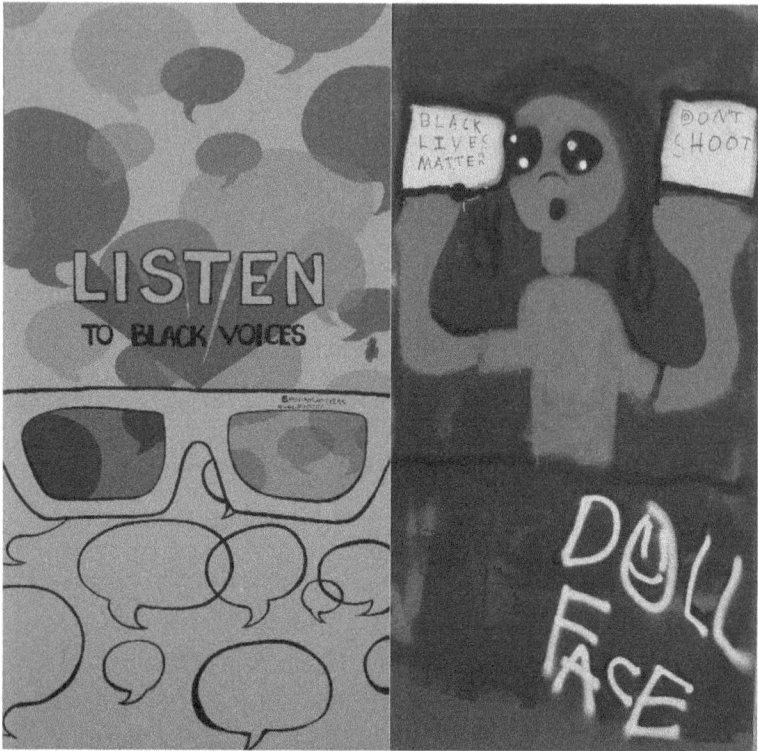

Get your Knee off Our Necks – Photo –

C.   OH, THAT 96 PERCENT
BY
DR. FRED MONDERSON

The brilliant Malcolm X put is best. During the Great Enslavement of African Americans, there were two kinds of Negroes. The House Negro comprised 4 percent and the Field Negro 96 percent of the enslaved population. The House Negro lived in the Master's House, wore his clothing, ate his food; what he left; enjoyed his health care and every privilege accorded the Master. The Field Negro did the strenuous labor on the plantation. He lived in a shack, ate sub-standard food and lacked adequate medical care. As such and as a result of the long train of physical, psychological and emotional abuse fueled by discriminatory and racist practices, scars on the psyche and person became implanted down through the perilous tunnel of racism, and discriminatory institutional behaviors resulting in social deprivation, most particularly lack of quality, even miseducation, despite struggles for social advancement and a variety of empowerment efforts, even political evisceration through disfranchisement and other forms of orchestrated voter suppression mechanisms, we arrive at the malady of COVID-19, Coronavirus, that has been a plague on the nation but most particularly on Brown and Black people.

The evidence is clear, at the end of slavery and in decades towards the end of the 19th Century, White American terrorism visited unspeakable horrors, lynchings, intimidation, share crop peonage, most particularly voter suppression through disfranchisement mobilization; yet, most significant, the national government demonstrated a refusal to protect the rights of the now freed citizens, tremendously oppressed in efforts to reinstate Southern, White Supremacy. While Blacks demonstrated a sense of loyalty to the Republican Party, because Abraham Lincoln freed the slaves, Republicans essentially turned their back in light of the said abuses. Thus, the Blacks turned to the Democratic Party in 1932 and have for the most part voted Democrat ever since.

In the heyday of Trumpian bombast, that age of "Only I," Donald Trump, despite being able to boast "There's my African American," coupled with a few lackeys such as Paris Dennard, Mark Burns, the what's his name preacher, Darrell, etc., all part of the House Negro contingent, Donald Trump wishfully stated, "By the end of my first term as President, 96 percent of African American will vote for me." It will certainly be foolish for him to say that in South Carolina. In fact, in accumulating the mountains of misstatements, he has probably forgotten such remarks. Nonetheless, he often boasts how much he has done for Blacks perhaps job-wise. In fact, while some Blacks got jobs, mostly with mops, buckets and as guards or waiters, these were generally cast offs as he raised the American boats. Look at any Trump presentation at a podium or on the Lawn of the White House and what you see is a sea of whites and a few Black butlers serving refreshments.

Trump was never concerned with the living conditions of Blacks, their health status and how they lack resistance as in case of the Carona-Virus Pandemic that is now wreaking havoc on this segment of the population. He may be aware they have the vote and are in significant numbers among America's military forces. How many Black senior

GET YOUR KNEE
OFF OUR NECKS

military officers has President Trump promoted in four years? Certainly not many, if any at all. Thus, much of this dereliction of duty towards the 96 percent he hoped would vote for him in 2020 is responsible for the condition that now persists. Sadly, even the meager gains in Black unemployment have vanished, given "last hired, first fired" syndrome. More important, however, "axle grease slick" Trump, like most conniving politicians who finally come around, will now say, by re-electing me your jobs will return. Its like, the enormous tax cut he and Mitch McConnell enacted from day one touting the enormous investments that will be made to benefit the working and other poor and none of this came to fruition. Nevertheless, savvy Americans are familiar with the cliché "first time shame on you; second time, shame on me!" The reality is, just as the Republican Party and associates of Donald Trump has fought Barack Obama as President, systematically orchestrated disfranchisement efforts to suppress the Black vote, blocked funding for Black relief efforts, more than sixty times voted to defund or eliminate the ACA or "Obamacare" that has benefitted so many Americans hungering for health care, Republicans, hope this constituency would forget past behaviors and enable them further. Fortunately, the have loyalists such as Sheriff Clarke, Allen West, Mark Burns, even Ben Carson, even that **Blacks for Trump 2020** idiot we often saw at his early rallies. These house Negroes have no place to go but Trump's backyard, not in his White House.

Equally important, these Negroes are used as bait on hooks to falsely convince the uninformed Black to vote for Trump in 2020. Fact is, all the important people, especially the Black ones, such as James Clyburn, Susan Rice, Tammy Beck worth, Bakari Sellers, Laura Coates, Keisha lance-Bottoms, Ben jealous, etc., say **VOTE BIDEN** not Trump, and be careful of Republican smear-filled and spiteful false ads and misinformation to nullify the Black vote. Watch out for Mr. West, he may very well be a Black Donald Trump Manchurian Candidate to confuse and siphon off Black votes from Biden. After all, he was already in Donald Trump's camp and its not too far a stretch, as a businessman, Kanye West may be at it again.

GET YOUR KNEE OFF OUR NECKS

d. JOE BIDEN IS NOT THE ENEMY!
BY
DR. FRED MONDERSON

How sad, the young voters who look to experts in media, even arm-chair commentators, are being misled big-time as these few "axe-grinders" seal the fate of so many. While Mitch McConnell may tell President Obama to "Shut his mouth" he won't tell those crucifying Biden to shut up because they're helping his agenda. As such, these comments…

The paper, *New York Post*, published four **Letters to the Editor** under the heading: "Taking Voters for Granted: Biden's 'Ain't Black' Gaffe by Storm Destro, Bayonne, New Jersey; Gary Schwartz, Trumbull, Connecticut; Alan Schumback, Manhattan; and Frank Ciofalo, Palm Coast Florida. This is certainly a wide-net of commentators, and interestingly enough, I read the letters several times searching for Pronouns as "I, Us, We," to imply these comments were by Black-Americans and these were none. Nevertheless, the implication is that all Black people endorse these comments on their behalf. No response was made on Biden's behalf, even though he recognized his statement to

279

FREDERICK MONDERSON

Charlemagne was inappropriate and apologized. The issue is conflated and confused. The real issue is who will Blacks vote for, who will win the 2020 election and how Blacks and the nation will fare, given Black folks have been and will always be a great part of the conscience of the American experiment as they continue to contribute to saving its soul.

One thing is certain, Mr. Trump must run on his record, past, Present and what he will project. Another certainty, if it is bad now, it will most certainly and unquestionably get worse by the time of the election. Nevertheless, however everyone spins it, the issue is, who will Blacks vote for in November 2020, will it be Joe Biden or Donald Trump and while we must consider Black interest, we must also consider Black History. This is significant as we should also remember, Malcolm reminded all, 'History is a good teacher' and even more important, as Dr. Martin Luther King laid it down, "Any man who will not stand for something will fall for anything." As such, whatever may be said, Black people have dignity, compassion, feelings, and oftentimes stand for right against wrong. This mindset is so powerful, like Christ on the Cross who pardoned that sinner, Blacks even pardon or forgive killers as Dylan Roof of the Mother Emanuel Massacre because they did not want to be burdened with the associated hate. But South Carolina is one incident of many. Yet still, despite the oppression, intimidation, lynching, and murder over the years! Therefore, are we to forgive and forget everything and everyone, over and over again. So, first of all and remembering, let's deal with the 'white elephant,' Donald Trump, in the room.

1.   For more than five years Donald Trump disrespected, harassed and flagellated Barack Obama over the 'Birther' falsity and this persisted throughout the entire two terms of Mr. Obama's Presidency. Four years into Donald Trump's own Presidency, he still castigates and tries to oppress Mr. Obama as if he was a piece of gum under his shoe.

2.   Donald Trump called protesting NFL players "Sons of Bitches." Today, while the NFL has essentially apologized, even suggesting teams should offer Kaepernick an opportunity to return to his sport. Even Donald Trump has come around, sort of, but he made his points falsely with his base.

3.   In one of is "Greatest Hits," Mr. Trump called out, "There's My African American over there" implying a Black person in the crowd, perhaps the only one there supported him. Strange, however, that man was on CNN denouncing Donald Trump for his racism, lack of leadership and abundance of lies!

4.   Claiming he has done more for all Black person than anyone else. "Pre-K-ish." Even Fannie

FREDERICK MONDERSON

Lou Hamer did more than Donald Trump for Black people. Trump even claims Black voters will like him more than they do President Obama. He should give us some of the stuff he smokes in the White House Bunker.

Get your Knee off Our Necks – Photo –

5.   Trump blames Democrats for problems in the Black community while advocating for more

protection and lack of accountability for the actions of the police.

6.   He championed Giuliani's police action that killed Sean Bell and others.

7.   He criticized Democrats for allowing problems in inner cities that affect Black citizens.

8.   He used misleading figures about Black unemployment and employment.

9.   Errol Lewis reminded of what Trump said of Abby Philips whom he said "asks stupid questions" About April Ryan, "Who doesn't know what the hell she is doing" and to Yamiche Alcindor "you ask racist questions."

10.   In response, Errol Lewis says of - "The three women -- all of them gifted, accomplished professionals -- will be covering politics long after Trump has left the White House." They join a long list of athletes, entertainers, journalists and politicians who Trump routinely attacks as "dumb," "not qualified," "low IQ," or some such insult.

All of this is contemporary and purportedly some Backs will forgive Trump but be reminded and hold it against Joe Biden for some legislative action he took some 30-years ago. At least, if Joe Biden wins the presidency as Barack Obama, Colin Powell and James Clyburn have given their support, we will see

FREDERICK MONDERSON

Black images behind Biden in any Photo-Op in comparison to Donald Trump's consistently all white associates. That is, except when he seems to pander to Black religious figures especially as if to co-opt them into supporting him. Fact is, Joe Biden is not the enemy, Donald Trump is the enemy of good government, good leadership, good empathy, the enemy of anti-racism and divisiveness. He trashes Black Lives Matter but supports Confederate statues and flags, nightmarish reminders of Black Slavery and treasonous division of the nation, death of Union soldiers and hoisting of Confederate flat that did not come from the Battlefield but were hoisted in defiance of Brown Board of Education of Topeka Kansas (1954) and the Civil Rights Movement to desegregate the nation. This is as James Clyburn recounted when Governor Haley removed the South Carolina flag following Dylan Roof rampant murder in the Mother Emanuel Cathedral in South Carolina.

GET YOUR KNEE OFF OUR NECKS

e. "THE BROKEN SYSTEM I INHERITED" BY DR. FRED MONDERSON

In the Coronavirus briefings on April 10, 2020, President Trump again flailed "The previous administration" about "The broken system I inherited." In the same breath in explaining efforts to combat the economic and health malady engulfing the nation, he equally remarked "we're getting along with the Democrats." Nonetheless, recognizing President Trump is exhibiting campaign mode of behavior during the White House Coronavirus briefings, his unrelenting attacks against his predecessor allows blind men to see the evil and insidious intent of such actions of the bloody trail he paved from Housing discrimination, Central park Five condemnation and Birther falsity, to unrelenting disparagement of a good man, we see

Mr. Trump for the little man that he is, as Lady Gaga has expressed, a "racist and fool."

Back in 2014, President Obama spoke to a "pandemic" on the horizon "within a 5-year to a decade and we must fix this" and so Donald Trump attacked "the previous administration" for leaving "the cupboard bare of incubators even though Obama left some 16,000 such Health Care devices to combat any impending pandemics but Donald Trump's anti-Black, anti-Obama lack of wisdom, poor leadership and blatant racist outlook grounded in Republican philosophy and mantra of "denying the Black guy a win," mentality dismantled this system just before it was needed. Sadly, he put nothing in place to prepare the nation. Today, we are far along in the devastating impact of the Virus on America and if only, did Donald Trump possess the ability to recognize wisdom in his predecessor he may have saved some of the evil his face represents today. Let's not forget Trump is a pathological liar. Lacking such a futuristic recognition and admonition was well-within the unrelenting Republican orchestrated full-court press against the first African-American President that began in 2008 with Mitch McConnell's marching orders resulting in his racist pronouncement, "I intend to make Barack Obama a one-term president." Added to this assault, the Republican "Party of No" blocking every legislative initiative of President Obama certainly contributed to the effort to make his presidency a failure. Much of this, Trump, washed out of ideas and lacking leadership continues to trumpet. Nevertheless, the brilliance of Mr. Obama thwarted the negativists and he is revered today among the great presidents.

Unquestionably, losers lose and winners win! And so, Mr. Obama persevered through courageous and thoughtful leadership, implementation of sound economic and financial policies and practice, exemplary and commendable role-modeling behaviors added to the unending prayers of those grandmothers bolstering the faith of Mr. Obama in those times of doubt.

Beginning with his racist "birther folly and inherent falsity" Mr. Trump, in nearly four years of his presidency, has invoked the name of Mr. Obama nearly one hundred times, blaming his predecessor for practically everything that has gone wrong with him, except the nearly 20,000 lies he himself has spoken. He seems to appeal to the old and tired anti-Obama racist of whom Mitch McConnell has been leading that pack of lemmings leading the nation over the cliff of human decency. Sadly, in Mr. Trump's alternative universe, he cannot see the mountain of lies and misstatements he has uttered, or the manner in which Putin, Kim, and Xi have played him "like a fiddle." He cannot see or smell the odious racist verbiage he constantly spouts even as he defends confederate flags and statues, relics of America's sordid past when traitors nearly destroyed the Union. He cannot see the nation loves

FREDERICK MONDERSON

Barack Obama and the more he invokes Obama's name, the larger he grows in stature. As for the envy of Mr. Obama that drives Mr. Trump, as the song says, "It Burns Inside!" Such denials are the *modus operandi* of "little men," members of Mr. Trump's cabal.

How sad that Mr. Trump's base ignores the racist banter and racism he encourages and connects this to their own viewpoint. Afterall, if someone speaks for you, you own what he says and sadly, Mr. Trump and the racists, white supremacists, KKK, men and women in red hats, etc., the world see as super racists and the face of America. More important, however, as President Trump ignores the Carona-Virus Pandemic that now targets "his base," so too, the issues Mr. Obama corrected when he assumed the presidency have been whittled away and the states now lack those protections. Every Obama achievement Donald Trump reversed, climate agreement, Iran Nuclear Deal, air and water safety, truth and effectiveness in government, integrity and empathy, constructive relationship with important allies were all in the interest of America's benefit. Instead, Donald Trump "fell in love" with Kim Jung Un, he "loves Putin," genuflects to Xi, adores Erdogan, and supports the Saudi Crown Prince who killed the journalist Khashoggi. We must now be concerned about the broken system, American institutions, Mr. Biden will inherit from Donald Trump's poor leadership. Afterall, John Bolton offered, "We may be able to

GET YOUR KNEE
OFF OUR NECKS

correct Trump's destruction of America's institutions over one term, but we may not survive two terms." Thus, Donald Trump must be defeated in the 2020 General Election.

f.   THE FORTUNA COOKIE
BY
DR. FRED MONDERSON

During the 2016 presidential campaign, a proud, more rightly arrogant, Donald Trump boasted, "If I shoot someone on Fifth Avenue, I would not lose a single vote!" This is criminal arrogance. Today, mayor De Blasio's intent to paint Black Lives Matter on 5th Avenue, a heartless Trump calls such action essentially criminal. Perhaps he did not because he so mesmerized so many, especially those who chose to wear red hats. This expose went unchallenged. Back then, Mr. Trump's nemesis, former President Barack Obama prophetically proclaimed among the highly charged election hoopla, "What if we are wrong." And, this too went unheeded. Today, after more than 130,000 Americans have died from Covid-19 on Mr. Trump's "watch," while not explicitly stating that characteristic arrogant line, he hopes and looks forward to being reelected on the same, "I won't lose a single vote" mantra. Sadly, a great many Americans, particularly Mr. Trump's "base" are ahistorical, unheeding and refuse to recognize his arrogance, condemnation and lies have increased manifold. Thank goodness, some Republicans led by Mr. Conway are fighting back.

During Mr. Obama's second term with Hillary Clinton as Secretary of State, the "Arab Spring" happened and so too "Benghazi" in which 4 Americans unfortunately lost their lives while executing their foreign policy mission. In response to this sad situation, Republicans orchestrated and executed a vendetta campaign of Committee hearings designed to embarrass and further contribute to the scattershot mandate of Mitch McConnell and his sycophants as well as outrageous "Tea Party" operatives' behaviors, all Knights of the "Party of No!" The principal executioner of this sinister vendetta campaign was Representative Trey Gowdy. Today, as the Republic stands seriously wounded, not so much by the current pandemic but the more sinister leadership or lack thereof, of Donald Trump, Mr. Gowdy is nowhere to be heard speaking on behalf of America and its long-standing and cherished values of integrity, leadership, moral courage and humanistic benevolence that earned this nation the respect of the world.

GET YOUR KNEE
OFF OUR NECKS

In ancient times, Diogenes Laurentius was once observed carrying a lit lantern at high-noon. Observers were confused and queried, why. He simply stated, "I'm looking for an honest man." Today, those sentiments fit Republicans who with their heads in the sand, ignore all that President Trump says and does.

Who could forget the courageous Captain Kirk! Of Star Trek fame, dispatching the perennial Klingon threat then see their ship subsequently amble crippled and aimlessly into the dark void of deep-space?

All Americans need be reminded, at the height of the French Revolution, the Englishman Edmund Burke was so outraged with the movement turning upon itself uttered those prophetic words, "The only thing necessary for evil to triumph is for good men to do or say nothing." While Mr. Trump likes to cast critical news reporting as "fake news" they see and point to wrongdoing by Mr. Trump and his associates. The fakes are really Trump and Republicans who "speak no evil, hear no evil, and see no evil," in the President's behavior.

Alas, the Gowdy bully, silenced, is now aimlessly adrift in the Klingon void of "faded glory" and he is there accompanied by "Waterloo" DeMint; "Joe the Plumber;" Allen West; "You Lie" Joe Wilson; "Lipstick on a Pig" Sarah Palin; Militias who massed before Obama; and the soon to be replaced

Majority Leader Senator Mitch McConnell and his ward, Donald Trump; even Attorney General William Barr, all the while, "Stupid Grassley" is hanging on by his fingernails, even as his associate Senator Lamar Alexander sadly etched his name in infamy in the American political and historical record book of anti-heroes.

Nevertheless, these "Sunshine" Patriots aside, when we consider the Donald Trump phenomenon, one has to believe the American people, the truly patriotic ones, are indeed keeping "score." In this regard, Mr. Trump recently responded to a Reporter's question, "I never take responsibility for anything," and this can refer to the more than 130,000 Americans who have unfortunately perished during his tenure as Commander and Chief Executive, the "Wartime President" who "surrendered." simply because at the dawn of the Pandemic he fiddled or perhaps golfed out and indoors.

Consider his character and given this unfolding calamity is bad, Mr. trump quickly extricated himself from responsibility. Now, while a vaccine appears to be on the horizon, "Good Ole Boy Trump" was quick to proclaim "I'm in charge" of the effort to create the cure. Americans remember the last guy who declared "I'm in charge" was quickly removed from his high-profile position as Secretary of State, that is Alexander Haig.

GET YOUR KNEE
OFF OUR NECKS

Thank goodness the *Washington Post* has a fact checker who clocked more than 20,000 lies and false statements Donald Trump fed the American people on the public airwaves which is more than 5000 lies per year so far. Mr. Trump lies faster than former New York Mets pitcher Nolan Ryan could pitch a fastball. The Declaration of Independence reminds, after "a long train of abuse, it is the duty" of the people to "abolish that government." As such, Americans must now "Liberate the White House." And, having moved from New York to Florida, Mr. Trump may eventually join "Moscow Mitch to reside overt here. We still wish them luck, in the proposed new digs!

g. "THANK YOU, LOU DOBBS!"
BY
DR. FRED MONDERSON

Thank you, Lou Dobbs for alerting us that President Donald John Trump is the greatest American president ever! Back in days of old, Howard Cosell once told the champ, "Mohammed Ali, you're not the man you used to be." As such, it's not too much of a leap to affirm, "You, Lou Dobbs, are not the man you used to be!" Perhaps, you're still the man you used to be because you appear to be just the same disgustingly faulty analyst. For, it seems not only as gray matter been tremendously expansive and retarding, but perhaps in your case you have chosen to see no evil, hear no evil and speak no evil.

However, and sadly, perhaps you are correct that Mr. Trump is the greatest liar to hold the Office of the Presidency. Even more, it cannot be considered honorable that a draft dodger aspired to the presidency to become Commander-in- Chief. Biden said, Trump "surrendered," when he could have stood up for the sanctity of the American flag which all soldiers fight under, he now hypocritically criticizes using false pretense as a badge of honor.

A significant approach of previous presidents has been carrot and stick. That is, carrots for allies and sticks for bad guys who threaten America. Your man uses sticks on America's allies and gives America's enemies carrots and candy; even falling in love with individuals who air videos of rockets landing on American soil and threated to do as much.

During periods of calamity and challenge to American emotional and psychological well-being, presidents have offered empathy and warmth to sooth the nation's ills and sadness. They have preached unity as a galvanizing force and rally cry. Mr. Trump on the other hand, offers cold ice and bombast, vicious tweets and threats to anyone who does not agree with him and considers them as the enemy. Imagine, calling the press the enemy. That means, even you old boy Lou, you too are the enemy, given you are in the Media.

GET YOUR KNEE
OFF OUR NECKS

Following the terrorist attack of September 11, 2001, the world stood in solidarity with the American nation recognizing America as a great champion of human values, truth and honesty. President George Bush then proposed the Invasion of Iraq to silence Weapons of Mass Destruction threats. The world said No! The President chose "To go it alone." This action soured the world's view of American, seriously affecting its relationships with allies. President Barack Hussein Obama; your man's nemesis perennially castigated in Trump's childish yet mean-spirited demeanor; deployed his infectious smile and secret weapon "Mighty Michelle." She floored the allies and even the nation's enemies took notice. They implored come visited again and often. And so, Mr. Obama brought allies back into the American fold. Your man, on the other hand, insulted the allies, praised the nation's virulent enemies, fell in love with others even giving them an elevated status on the world stage. While the allies implored Obama to return after his visit, they asked Mr. Trump to hurriedly leave and don't come back. The enemies insisted your man Trump come visit so as to play him as they did, giving them much needed respectability and he got little or nothing in return, except perhaps, their fiddle.

Claiming to be a wartime president, while acting like the Private General Patton kicked, your man's 2020 Presidential opponent thought him "An absolute fool." Your man was so hypocritical taking credit for Obama's economic and financial foundation in the present recovery plan, now "Mother nature" has slapped your man for his arrogance, destroying the economic foundation he falsely claimed credit for and visited upon him and America a pandemic virus beyond proportion. That "absolute fool," refuses to acknowledge and manfully apply leadership in this pandemic malady and the tumultuous expressions playing out across the country because of the death of one Black man, George Floyd, who touched the world.

Your "Greatest President Ever" wishfully thinks there will be a "V-shaped upturn of the Economy" for him to be re-elected but this will not happen for some time. Remember, there is no Obama economic foundation to build on and there are some 40 million unemployed. Add this to the virus and the 120,000 deaths that resulted from your man sleeping at the wheel, all because of failed leadership. Or, was he playing golf as the virus began to spread, or fiddling as America burns? Then again, according to his regular refrain, "I don't know…." Be careful, toe the line r he may exclaim, "Lou Dobbs, I never heard of him."

GET YOUR KNEE
OFF OUR NECKS

h. OBAMA FOR BIDEN!
BY
DR. FRED MONDERSON

For many observers, President Obama was supposed to endorse his deputy to fill the office they both administered. Some years ago, there was one notable exception to this sort of natural development. That is, the Brooklyn, New York, Boro President Howard Golden, "How He Go" failed to endorse his Deputy Boro President Jeanette Gadsen as she sought to be elected, to the position he vacated. Ms. Gadsen was African-American but

FREDERICK MONDERSON

Mr. Golden endorsed Marty Markowitz, a member of his Jewish ethnic group.

On the other hand, former President Barack Obama remained on the sidelines during the shortened Democratic Presidential Primary preferring not to show partiality even though some candidates used his image in their campaign messaging. Still, the president chose not to favor any of the many democratic candidates giving the public a chance to vet those seeking the nomination. However, once the primary campaign was aborted, forced by the coronavirus pandemic, the frontrunner, Joe Biden became the declared presumptive nominee and the last holdout, Senator Bernie Sanders abandoned his quest, then Biden's position became somewhat solidified. Even more significant, before the abrupt end of the campaign, one by one withdrawn candidates began endorsing Joe Biden and this sort of forced Sanders' capitulation and his ultimate endorsement of Biden. Subsequently, Mr. Obama came out in support of Joe Biden.

All of the above, notwithstanding, there was an even more pressing reason, it appears, why Mr. Obama chose to support Mr. Biden. It appears to be the unqualified and urgent necessity to remove President Donald Trump from the White House and as head of the American government because of displayed poor or lack of leadership, among the litany of his many faults. Naturally, some may argue, Obama had a bone to pick because of the

GET YOUR KNEE
OFF OUR NECKS

"Birther" harassment and more particularly how he campaigned for Hillary Clinton, though that proved ineffective. Nevertheless, as is customary, persons are almost always given a chance to redeem themselves in what-ever position they find themselves. This Mr. Trump could or did not want to do.

The Declaration of Independence has been viewed as one of the most significant documents and developments in the history of the Western World. Not only did the Declaration enshrine the immortal words, "We hold these truths to be self-evident, that all men are created equal, that they are endowed by their creator with certain inalienable rights and are entitled to life, liberty, and the pursuit of happiness;" but even more important it accused the British King George III of committing "a long train of abuse and usurpations!"

The Age of Obama is uniquely exceptional in this country. The first African-American to be nominated to be its standard bearer by a major political party, he campaigned resolutely and was surprisingly elected as the first Black to win the Presidency. He inherited a nation in economic and financial crisis, fighting two foreign wars while economic chaos was the order of the day. Rolling up his sleeve and delving deep into the myriad of problems facing the nation, this man possessing elegance of mind and nobility of spirit, brought the nation back to standards of normalcy. Yet, throughout the vicissitudes of Republican disrespect, sabotage and uncooperative behaviors, not to discount threats to his personal well-being, Mr. Obama finished his term on a high note and is today regarded with tremendous respect worldwide. Even more significant, despite all that was said and done to him, Mr. Obama shrugged it off saying, "I know politics is a contact sport!"

For decades, Donald Trump had aspirations for the White House, but he could not get the needed traction, despite his wealth and social aspirations. Lo and behold, in Mr. Obama's meteoric rise to the presidency, Mr. Trump discovered the racist

GET YOUR KNEE
OFF OUR NECKS

"Birther nugget" and vigorously and unbelievably polished it into the Presidency.   Whether its reflection or "Monday Morning Quarterbacking" we have come to peel back the smelly onion regarding the men and plots that manifested as the little minds tried to tie Gulliver, light years ahead in intellectual acuity, political persona and social gregariousness that made his Lilliputian adversaries seem like charlatans, that they truly are.

Malcolm X often reminded, "History is a great teacher" for as we look back on thought, deeds, and actions,   the shallow insidiousness of men who should be pillars of consciousness, paragons of good government and intellectual standard-bears, these individuals prove to be wood being bitten by wood-ants.   For   example,   recently   Donald   Trump unleashed one of his defection gems in accusing the former president of creating "Obamagate." From the little we know so far, the language Obama used in referring to the claimed situation was so perfect, he made **Webster's Dictionary** look like child's play.   After all, a constitutional scholar who was elected as the first African-American President, Mr. Obama demonstrated great love and respect for the Presidency and so was able to exit unscathed to later be hailed as a great statesman and icon. Compare this with the foulmouthedness of such as "Waterloo" DeMint; ""Stupid Grassley; "You lie" Wilson; "Lipstick on a Pig" and "Palling around with Terrorists" Sarah Palin; the "Most dangerous man in

America" Allen West; and "Show me the Birth Certificate," Donald Trump.

Now, having survived the long train of Republican abuses, and front row witness to the dirty tricks demonstrated by Donald Trump, his lies, abuses, undue influence through his office to subvert the law in interest of his associates, some call cronies, disrespect for America's strongest allies while the Office of the Presidency supports the aspirations, not simply of Donald Trump but of every tin-horn dictator worldwide, even Stevie Wonder could see the White House needs to be liberated. Even Republicans of stature have noted Mr. Trump needs to be packing on November 3, 2020 for he will destroy what American institutions he has not damaged so far. Still, is disgusting negativist and lawlessness has breached ever portal and infected every institution form Inspector General to Department of Justice, not to mention the United states Senate, the world's greatest deliberative body!

Donald Trump, a man of low IQ, is a divider, race baiter who hides between the mantra "I am the least racist person in the world." His is a sordid history of racist behaviors, from his refusal o rent to Blacks in New York, refusing to have Black men count his casino money, his attack on the "Central Park Five," now the "Exonerated Five," let's not get into his Birther falsity, abuse of Black women, particularly the four congressional representatives, calling African countries "Shithole," and the fact he so stupid not to realize, the *Washington Post* has clocked him at nearly 22,000 lies or false, even misleading statements. Now, if history is any barometer, given a second term, Donald Trump will destroy this great nation beyond repair, perhaps even the world as the insane contemplate. That is why, among other things Barack Obama and a great number of retired military and law enforcement officials agree, Joe Biden is the man to heal the nation and repair institutions Trump trampled upon as he has the Constitution, the document that upholds not just the rule of law but the fundamental principles that made this nation admired and great.

BIDEN IS THE MAN!

FREDERICK MONDERSON

i.   RUDY AND THE ART OF THE CON
BY
DR. FRED MONDERSON

People have a tendency to ignore what they do not want to notice. At the Republican National Convention, amidst the bells and whistles hoopla, former New York City May Michael Bloomberg assessed the Trump candidacy by stating, "I know a con when I see one!"   No one listened! When Barack Obama exhorted, "What if we are wrong?" not many paid attention as well. Caught up in the titillating melodic sounds of the Pied Piper leading his followers along a path not clearly defined. Friend and foe insisted, "Give Mr. Trump a chance he is a businessman, not a politician. The hope was, the office, because of its significance in the responsibility it represents will transform the new president into a true leader of ethical, caring and

304

GET YOUR KNEE
OFF OUR NECKS

concerned consciousness, gentleman of legal and moral optimum behavior.

When James Clyburn described the 2016 Presidential contest as "The most consequential election of our time," some ignored those prophetic sounds of alarm, some listened; African-Americans especially those believed "Puffy Combs" over Clyburn in his insistence to "Hold the vote!" This Puffy, Sean Combs, Puff Daddy, P. Diddy, Diddy, which is the real one and why does this give him the authority to prognosticate on the vote, is an unsolved question. After all, Puffy is a "Party animal" and Clyburn is in the lion's den at the nation's political dynamics. Nonetheless, all things being equal, we ended up with Donald Trump as president.

By James Clyburn "yardstick" despite Hillary Clinton's indiscretions, African-Americans would have been seen in her company in any photo-op public display. What we see is an "all white" team of perhaps "very fine people" behind Mr. Trump.

So, Donald Trump became president. His was an agenda somewhat different from previous chief executives in that he consistently looked like "The China in the Bull shop!"

Dismantle, even abolish the Affordable Care Act, mischievously labeled "Obamacare." Coming to the presidency in his expertly tailored "Birther outfit," for four years on a daily basis, Donald Trump lambasted Barack Obama, his administration and his personnel, none of whom were associated with the slightest inappropriate behavior. While, on the other hand, the trump administration and associates have been muddied in the morass of lies, guilty pleas, indictments, jailings and abuse of practically everyone from Pope to Pauper. Yet, sadly, Republican lawmakers and political supporters, particularly the evangelical right have remained silent while the soul, conscience and morality of the nation sank into virulence of Trump's ineptitude, bombast and obfuscation, even as he insulted the nation's staunchest allies but seems to owe loyalty to Putin. He wants his minions to kiss his ring as he presides over America's descent from the mountain top of respectability to depths of unthinkable ridicule. Clearly historical commentary will have much to say about Republican political minions who think they're whales.

Nearly a year ago, the Trump circus initiated a plan that recognized Jerusalem as Israel's capital, a delicate high-wire act, previous presidents had skillfully danced. Military might coupled with arrogance creates a scenario where too many are seen as "chewing gum" beneath the sole of an oppressor's feet. Ipso facto, Donald Trump, Rudy Giuliani, and the "Good looking rascal" rolled out their new mantra of "The chosen one!" While this winter is not fully aware in the "good looking rascal's role in, both Rudy and Donald trumpeted

GET YOUR KNEE
OFF OUR NECKS

the mantra and began looking heavenward "to justify their chosen one" con and falsity, yet seemingly seeking "divine approval."

Long pass the three-card monte con with no ball under any shell, Mr. Trump continued to tout "the enemy," "Wall Street" and "low unemployment rates." Whether bookies, inveterate gamblers, even ballplayers know streaks come to an end. And so, Wall Street, the economy and high employment all came crashing down amidst a pandemic that that slapped America in the face, and threatens the American way of life far into the future. Sadly, t he Trump magician has not been able to invoke to "Chosen One," "Divine Connection" mantra he so assioudisly foisted on the American people now that "Mother nature has chosen to rebel. Or, is it the gods are angry at Trump's blasphemy as he unrolled his 15th con job? Still, the American people must pay for his lack of leadership, arrogance and evil ways.

FREDERICK MONDERSON

j. OLYMPUS HAS INDEED FALLEN
BY
DR. FRED MONDERSON

Yes, Olympus has indeed fallen but not to foreign terrorists but a home grown psychological, emotional and ethical wrecking ball in the person of President Donald Trump, particularly in the vocabulary used to describe the man and his leadership. For nearly two and a half centuries, America unfolded two of the most potent documents that have not simply stood the test of time but have also influenced men, movements and nation states to mold their future political action. More important, these two documents remind us of the impact of words on expectations and actions.

GET YOUR KNEE
OFF OUR NECKS

History reminds us, as the French Revolution raged, consuming its many theorists and political actors, the Englishman Edmund Burke in Reflections on the Revolution in France (1793) wrote the immortal words: "The only thing necessary for evil to triumph is for good men to do or say nothing!" Today, evil has triumphed in the Presidency of Donald John Trump! However, there is enough blame to go around that Mr. Trump owes his lack of credibility to a whole host of issues, man of his own doing; but equally important no "Guardrails" in the persons of Republican operatives who themselves have equally lost credibility in their inability to call out or correct Mr. Trump for his lies, fraudulent claims and vindictive and poor leadership

Attorney General William Barr is a principal in tis gaggle not so much from poor leadership of the Justice Department but equally for is acting as the President's lawyer rather than t he people's top law enforcement officer.

The captain of this "ship of fools," none other than Senate Majority Leader Mitch McConnell, who from as early as 2008 with the election of Barack Obama as the first African American President, began to show his true colors. Then, perhaps acting on marching orders from his "handlers" McConnell began driving in the wrong direction of the highway of history. In this "fool's errand," Mr. McConnell's "open mouth" stated: "I intend to make Barack Obama a one-term president." Now, after two terms of memorable service and well-liked by the American people; yet, if we falsely admit Barack Obama made a ton of mistakes which, this early he could not have made, then we are left with the only tangible fact, the President is Black! Naturally, The New York Times Expose of October 6, 2013, commenting on Mr. Obama's 2012 re-election entitled, "A Plot long in the making" recounted Mitch McConnell and the several Republican operatives who plotted against the Obama Presidency, his re-election campaign, and the many legislative initiatives he proposed. What Mr. McConnell could not achieve through political manipulation he probably achieved through prayer, if he ever does, praying for a "great white hope" to "take back our country." Lo and behold, this errand was undertaken to bring back "Truth, Justice and the American way!" Instead, Mr. McConnell got Donald Trump and truck loads of LIES, racial hatred, division, weak leadership, not providing guardrails against foreign entanglements in the American political and social process, even injuries to American lives while he could not deliver on important foreign policy, even domestic promises. He got "Conservative judges!" or, as Trump likes to call them, "My judges!"

The moral authority on the world stage that characterized America among nation states, the presidential timber that so embodied great American leaders, the honesty, integrity, empathy and unifying symbols the nation's highest office exemplified

GET YOUR KNEE
OFF OUR NECKS

were dashed by the crassness Trump rule, his poor leadership, came to represent. An un relenting crusade of hatred and animosity towards his immediate successor Barack Obama, ill-will towards anyone who dared to look at him, the most vile treatment towards America's long-standing allies, seeking to reduce American government to his own fiefdom, not to discount his own mountain of lies, even dangling pardons to anyone who remotely could testify against him and exemplifying a vice-grip and sharp Sword of Damocles against any in his party who broke ranks, even if they spoke the truth, came to characterize the nature of business according to Trump.

www.ingramcontent.com/pod-product-compliance
Lightning Source LLC
Chambersburg PA
CBHW060249100426
42742CB00011B/1686